REFLUX+

For Rudy R —

with the very best —

[signature] 2018

MALCOLM MC NEILL

REFLUX+

SOME THINGS JUST WON'T STAY DOWN

APOPHENIA

REFLUX+

the complete collection of essays published

in

PARAPHILIA MAGAZINE

in the U.S.

and

INTERNATIONAL TIMES

in the U.K.

2013 - 2018

I am indebted to **Dire McCain** at *Paraphilia*
and **Heathcote Williams** and **Claire Palmer** at
International Times for making that possible.

First published in 2018

by

APOPHENIA

ISBN-13: 978-0692066041

AN ILLUSTRATED MENAGERIE OF SACRED COWS
AND INCONVENIENT TRUTHS RECONSIDERED

CONTENTS

LOVERBOY

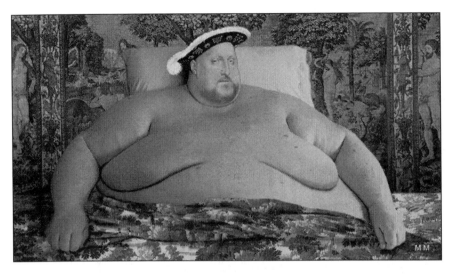

"…Hollywood started cranking out princesses like sausages…"

Sultry, French princess Isabella leans down to the dying king Edward and whispers in his ear ... *"A child who is not of your line grows in my belly. Your son will not sit long on the throne... I swear it."* Her fey, cuckolded husband - the *next* king Edward - strains to hear her, as the audience squirms with delight. What an exquisitely saucy comeuppance! The crafty William Wallace - our own lovable Mel, who was soon to be formally disemboweled - had managed to slip a Freedom bun into the royal oven! Mel Gibson and Sophie Marceau going at it! Think of it! What an image! ... and what a remarkably tricky piece of fucking.

History tells us that Edward I died in 1307, but Isabella of France would not marry the unwitting Edward II until the *following* year - when she was 12 years old. There is nothing particularly remarkable about that, the dying king had also married a 12 year old, who produced 10 children by the time she was 22. What's tricky is that William Wallace was executed in 1305 - *three years earlier.* In order for the scene to play out, Mel would have had to knock up little Sophie when she was 9, and at the time of her revelation, she would have been more than two YEARS pregnant.

Without sex, there would of course *be* no history, but that would be sex in a particular order and between people who actually existed. According to the movie *Braveheart,* it was the love of another woman - Wallace's equally comely wife - that set him off on his ill-fated rampage in the first place. It was her murder that initiated the sequence of events that would lead to all-out war with the English, the ultimate independence of Scotland and his own untimely demise. *History,* however, tells us next to nothing about Wallace himself much less the woman in question – certainly whether or not she looked like a *Victoria's Secret* model.

Thwarted love is also the impetus for the monumental exploits of Spartacus, played by Kirk Douglas. When the woman of *his* heart, Jean Simmons, is taken from him, he also goes on the rampage and takes on the source of his own oppression - Rome. History indeed appears to repeat itself: both Spartacus and Wallace lose exceptionally tasty squeezes up front, both rally their forces around the idea of Freedom, both are graphically executed and both are vindicated by their women folk: lovers who deliver them children posthumously to trump the powers that be and bring Freedom to bear. As with Wallace, history reveals hardly anything about Spartacus besides his name, uprising and defeat. There is no record at all of any 'babes' or babies.

In *Braveheart* these pivotal sexual encounters involve shadowy glimpses of breasts, bottoms and fingers set to a poignant 'romantic' musical score. In *Spartacus* they're not shown at all. When female slaves are paired off with gladiators in their cells to relieve them of their pent up frustrations, whatever sexual shenanigans may be forthcoming, are expressed in silence. When Jean Simmons bathes naked in a stream, she lays on her back with a determined foreground fern doggedly obscuring her breasts. In both films, sex is sensitively depicted or simply implied.

In the thirty years between the making of *Spartacus* and *Braveheart*, very little changed in that regard, but in the next twenty five it would change dramatically - along with the historical embellishments needed to justify it. Whereas historical movies may have little or nothing to do with historical events, they throw real light on the history of audience expectations when it comes to Romance and the "old in/out".

The Working class English have an expression - *"Whenever you look up, there's the queen's ass."* In a monarchy there's only so far you can go. But when Lady Diana Spencer showed up, that perspective changed. Monarchy was still monarchy, but that ass suddenly called for a lot more attention. Our Di, "The People's Princess", was *real* - in fact she was *hyper* real. She was *fairytale* come true. With Diana, the monarchies of *fiction* had seemingly become a monarchy of *fact*...

A shy young kindergarten teacher, is whisked away to a life of glamour and riches by a real life Prince Charming, produces two lovely heirs, is spurned by their father, sets out to save the world, is loved by all, and then is tragically killed - or was it murdered? Diana showed that with modesty, sincerity and love in your heart, it was possible to acquire untold wealth, get to wear a crown *and* assert yourself as a woman... but being a woman she could be used, abused and discarded. She wasn't just a woman, she was WOMAN and women the world over loved her for it - women the world over from 5 to 95. Diana was a heaven sent Golden Goose, a marketing wet-dream come true. She was Royalty, Fashion, Rock and Roll and Sex rolled into one. The 'Romance' of kings and queens, would make money like never before.

Hollywood started cranking out princesses like sausages. George Lucas even introduced a queen to Star Wars - an equally modern babe, equally determined, equally obsessed with getting gussied up, and with as much vitality as her dead role model. Royal families appeared in every movie theater, every bookstore, and on every television, all of them sexy, all of them fabulously beautiful. And finally, along came our Henry, that lovable, English "royal rogue", who sausaged more princesses than you could shake a stick at.

The Tudors is a "Period Drama", an epic reenactment of the larger than life and times of King Henry VIII: Opulent palaces and gardens, fabulous costumes and interiors, and all the pageantry and spectacle of monarchy, unfold against the backdrop of 16th century intrigue and conflict. Scenes are lavishly staged, art directed and choreographed, to evoke wealth, glamour and power, and lit to create a moody sensual environment ideal for plotting and sexual cavorting. Dialogue mimics a 'meaningful' Shakespearean style, evoking wit and insightfulness but conveying sentiments more in line with the concerns of modern day soap opera. Female characters are preoccupied with marriage, clothes, sexual infidelities, and babies, while men engage in the manly pursuits of political scheming, galloping around on horseback, eating, drinking, fighting and fucking.

In other TV melodramas, such as *Downton Abbey*, sexual interactions are known to the audience but not shown. In *The Tudors*, sex scenes are relentless and explicit. The effect is a Beauty Pageant on steroids: Female 'contestants' are introduced in elaborate costumes and jewelry to announce their resumes and intentions, then brought back later to take them off. Unlike the simple 'swimsuit' routine, any female new comer to the show, will in no time, first make much ado about revealing her breasts, then quickly get fully naked, throw the legs up and get down to business.

Henry is played by a buff young stud in keeping with his prowess as a lover - his wives, by healthy, attractive, mostly young women. The actual monarch's size increased significantly over time, but this is not reflected at all by his fictional counterpart. Whereas Henry expanded to land-whale proportions, the fictional Henry maintains his trim, soccer player physique throughout. The only overt physical disability his sexual partners have to contend with, is an unpleasant ongoing ulcer on his leg caused by a jousting accident in his youth. This is more a justification for his occasional crankiness than an obstacle to be addressed during sex. Organizing sensuality around the overall constraints of such a partner would have required extremely innovative, feminine guile - especially given the life or death nature of the project. Instead we are presented with the same old, entirely predictable, 'perfect body', in/out clichés.

There were a lot of things about our Henry that were unpleasant by modern standards - or any other standards for that matter - all of which would have added a certain poignancy to the prospect of personal and sexual interaction. His partners on occasions must have experienced a degree of apprehension, if not outright terror as he bore down upon them. *"Henry the Eighth, by the Grace of God, King of England, France and Ireland, Defender of the Faith and of the Church of England and also of Ireland in Earth Supreme Head"* could be a nasty son of a bitch.

In terms of character, he was vain, irascible, cruel, despotic, obese and *'right'* - according to divine dispensation. He dumped the Pope in Rome in order to become Pope in England, assuming the prerogatives of divinity and continuing with the worst excesses of cruelty, intolerance and fraud espoused by the original. He murdered thousands of his own subjects, including women and children, had no qualms about hideously torturing and burning detractors alive, confiscated property to finance wars for his own aggrandizement, and ramped up the Enclosure of the Common land to get the ball rolling on the privatization of nature. His sense of intellectual stature was expressed outwardly by his physical size, achieved by a lifetime of compulsive eating. His meat consumption was staggering; he drank alcohol in some form or other from morning 'til night. *And* he murdered his wives.

In terms of physics, he might be described as an ongoing series of explosive mental and digestive events occurring within a dangerously overbearing structure weighing in at more than 350 pounds. As with most people of his time, a structure that was rarely washed. He would have been a formidable challenge to the hardiest of women.

Rather than gasping "*I'm coming*", a land mass of such magnitude might conceivably have announced it was " *about to arrive*" - or had some appointed official announce it for him - and even clean up after, like the "*Groom of the Stool*" who wiped the royal backside. Given the king's diet and girth it must have been a daunting task, yet this seemingly lowest of functions was considered one of the highest of honors. Very few were entitled to such pampering. In contrast to the opulence of its fixtures and fittings, restroom facilities at the palace were rudimentary and descended in scope according to station. As a commoner, Anne Boleyn probably had to wipe her own bum when she first arrived at court, prompting one to (briefly) consider whether her queenly prerogative was rescinded once she was up for the chop.

Her sister, as it happened, was the first to get a crack at the King. In the show, when they meet, she curtseys in front of him, rummages around in his codpiece, and nonchalantly starts tongue-basting the contents. One way or another, both sisters it seems, were destined to give head. Their father had previously pimped out his underage daughters to the French court, but apparently unhappy with the dividends, had decided to give Henry a pop. Underage girls are a staple of monarchy, after all - the best money can buy. It's *Tradition* my dear! Most of the time, the ladies were more than happy to go along with it. Wouldn't you?

But Historical fiction is concerned with money not facts. Facts are the convenient hook on which to hang fiction in order to seduce an audience into spending - either directly through merchandising, or inversely through advertising. Tudors' writer Hirst was very forthright: *"This is an example of history as a commodity; ... what would ultimately sell, in terms of audience figures, commissions and later sales from downloads and DVDs... if certain historical facts had to be left by the wayside, then so be it."*

It is simply the way of things: In order to make a return on investment, history must become entertainment; fact must become fiction. Our OWN PAST is just one more part of the *environment* to be plundered in the interest of profit.

It is a lazy kind of fiction, in that the most difficult part of the literary process is the invention of believable situation and character. With historical fiction this requires no effort at all, since they exist as historical fact.

They function like Ken and Barbie dolls to be dressed in comfortably contemporary mores and dialogue to reinforce a contemporary media/advertising mindset. Ideally, to add to the coercion, they are animated by already known, celebrity actors behaving according to fan expectations. It is a dolls and dollhouse mindset of make believe, wishful thinking and "wouldn't it be nice if"; a statement of dissatisfaction, petulant almost, that actual history just isn't good enough. *"We weren't going for the fat look"* said writer Hirst, as if it were an affectation of sorts, a kind of fashion statement that can be changed like simply putting on a new outfit. *"You have to make Henry for an audience today otherwise they're going to be bored."* said actor Rhys Meyers. Bored that is, with who we are, and who we really were.

Shakespeare was one of the first to use historical fiction in this manner - and he used it to similar ends. Turning history into entertainment glamorized his aristocratic and royal patrons and promoted the idea of England's rise to empire. It also paid the rent; Willy the Shake certainly knew *"...whereupon his bread was't buttereth."* Embellishment, exaggeration and outright lies all combined to support the powers that be - and it worked: the Empire took off and lasted five hundred years. Sex was not presented overtly, more as saucy interludes of innuendo. There would be no women with their legs up on stage in Tudor times, simply because women were not *allowed* on stage. The great female characters - Ophelia, Cordelia, Desdemona, Juliet and Lady Macbeth etc, - were all played by men. There *were* no tits on Titania.

But Shakespeare's blurring of fact and fiction continues to skew modern perceptions of historical characters. The real Henry V was probably nowhere near as wonderful, Macbeth nowhere near as bad.

Richard III, the murderous, scheming hunchback has suffered an opprobrium that has lasted centuries and is only now being redressed. No one reads Shakespeare as history, but the mish mash of fact and fiction he created endures. The question becomes then: who is orchestrating the embellishments and falsehoods now, and in the interests of which future empire?

The men and women who actually participated in the monarchy of Henry VIII had *unique* circumstances to contend with. They demonstrated the process by which the human endeavor endures, the process to which we are always in debt. History as commodity focuses entirely on what we've got, at the expense of what it really took to get it. It is an insult to the billions of human beings who experienced - and *suffered* - history as fact.

The women of Tudor times had no organized health care, no doctors, no dentists, no Ob/Gyn, no practical knowledge of infection and disease, no anesthetics, no sanitation, no running water, no *drinking* water, no bathrooms, no deodorants, no tampons, no health clubs, no yoga mats, no anti-depressants to help cope, yet they had to interact with men and other women to achieve exactly the same results as they do today. Young women under those conditions, coming to terms with a dangerously vain, supremely privileged, 350-pound, drunken carnivore with an erection, show true 'worth'. Such an idea is almost incomprehensible to us. It is truly amazing, but presenting them as beautiful contemporary women, in contemporary terms, interacting with a 'handsome' young contemporary male makes their achievement meaningless.

"*One owes respect to the living, but to the dead one owes only the truth.*" said Voltaire. We are unable to do that, simply because it costs too much. They must instead make do with glamorous falsehoods because those are the only things that make a profit - and reinforce the status quo. The political process is informed by historical Fact not historical Fiction. Those who do not study Fact will suffer a governance of Fiction. The purpose of Mass Media is to make sure they are in the majority.

ABRACADAVER

"...naked dead bodies engaged in all kinds of bizarre activities..."

Public executions have always been well attended. Road accidents cause rubber necking traffic jams. A neighbor across the street who undresses in the window can inspire investing in a telescope. Voyeurism – wanting to see someone naked, have sex, or die without them seeing you - is a fundamental human propensity. Films, television, and newspapers thrive on that account. Expanding on the tradition is Gunther Von Hagens, a German entrepreneur who has organized the idea into an all-encompassing *"Barnum and Bailey goes to the Morgue"* type event featuring naked, dead bodies engaged in all kinds of bizarre activities. Brought back to life as it were, in an extravaganza he calls *Bodyworlds*.

He presents his characters as medical wonders, revealing aspects of the body hitherto unseen by the public at large. They allow laymen and medical students alike an unprecedented view of its workings and construction. *Bodyworlds* he tells us, takes the endeavors of Vesalius and Leonardo to their ultimate conclusion. Blow-ups of their illustrations line the walls to confirm the idea.

It is a claim that is hard to refute. Few people have seen a complete stranger without their clothes on, even fewer one without his or her *skin* on. Skin, particularly facial skin, defines an individual. To remove it renders them entirely anonymous. Their bodies can be studied from an inch away without the slightest inhibition. A group of Spanish speaking ladies ahead of me demonstrated this by taking it in turns to squeeze the penis of one of the exhibits – then giggling hysterically afterwards. It's possible a few artists and medical students will appreciate being able to see the origin of *flexor carpi ulnaris*, but the ladies seem to be more what the show is about. They are also what makes it unsettling.

As far as anatomical insights go, the dried out shrunken musculature only approximates its original form. It looks - and as the ladies can attest - feels like beef jerky, which basically it is - the human equivalent at least. It lacks moisture, warmth and above all vitality. Watching the women laughing alongside brings the fact sharply into focus. We are really nothing like this at all. The initial wonder and voyeuristic thrill is quickly replaced by a kind of despair.

Von Hagen's efforts do not reveal the wonder of the body so much as they evoke the sad inconsequence of there no longer being any-*body* in it; the vacated premises as indicative of life as the ruins of a burned out building. Painting it up and putting a flowerpot in the window, simply reinforces the idea. The effect is to divert our attention from the things that are there, to the things that aren't, i.e. the original occupants. It prompts us to wonder how their bodies ended up in such a state.

We are not told who they were, but we can assume they weren't particularly 'significant'. People of means don't allow their earthly remains to be exploited in this manner, certainly not the kind of people in the audience. They are mostly diminutive bodies, suggesting ethnic types from places where trade of this kind is ethically less inhibited and more prompted by necessity. An ongoing anonymity, that further subtracts from the notion of celebrating life. Compounding the feeling are the sentimental posturings their bodies have been forced to adopt in their absence. Demeaning portraits completely antithetical to the heroic statuary of people who *do* achieve 'significance' in their lifetimes.

Utilizing a complex embalming process, called "Plastination", Von Hagens dismantles, distorts and rearranges his cadavers into fanciful 'lifelike' poses. To heighten the life/death *"ambiguity"*, as he puts it, he then adds various props - glass eyes for example, the same trick that makes stuffed animals appear life-like or children's dolls. And as if they were dolls, the good doctor then adds wigs, hats, cigarettes and fake pubic hair to increase the 'realism'.

A flayed corpse, described as' Winged Man" has been disassembled then reassembled in a way that stretches the body horizontally. In keeping with the title, the musculature has been detached and flared out to evoke the idea of flight. To heighten the illusion, the arrangement has then been placed on a revolving turntable. In seeming contradiction to the idea however, it has been topped off with a white fedora. A hat – we are told - *"further narrows the gap between life and death."*

Even without props, the arrangement of many of the figures is equally sentimentally contrived.

One tableau is dedicated to the circulatory system. The Plastinated blood vessels alone, remain to define the shapes of their former owners, a family group, in which the 'wife' has her arm around her 'husband's' waist, and he supports 'their child' on his shoulders. A happy child clearly, since its two tiny thumbs are raised. Without question these three human beings were in no way related in life. Assembling their physical remains in this way engenders a complicated mix of feelings – none of them joyful. A human being defined by its blood vessels does prompt a kind of wonderment, but the remains of a dead child arranged like this immediately cancels it out. The voyeurism short-circuits, comes out the other side as it were.

The most blatantly kitsch and by virtue of her context, most titillating exhibit, is a pregnant woman - the star of the show without question. She and a half-dozen fetuses in beakers have a room to themselves, an area designed and lit like a shrine. It's a place for spiritual contemplation as it were, since sex, birth and death are all present here.

We are informed before entering that the woman we are about to see, had a terminal illness that she knew could possibly claim her life and that of her child before she gave birth. In the likelihood of such an event, she had consented to donate herself and her child to be preserved for exhibition. It is an incredibly poignant scene to envision: a woman simultaneously contemplating death and the joy of motherhood while a stranger anticipates the possibilities should the former be the case. It is a terrible confluence of tragedy and opportunism.

We find her remains reclining on a steel table, her skin removed and her belly split open to reveal her hard discolored organs and gray unborn child. One arm has been placed behind her head like a woman lounging beside a swimming pool. The skin has been removed from her breasts but the erect nipples remain.

Everything after that pales by comparison.

• A flayed soccer player leaps to catch a real soccer ball with one hand while his organs fly in the opposite direction - a dilemma for any goalkeeper.

• A man whose musculature has been stretched to gigantic proportions pedals a suitably-enlarged, badly-built bicycle while wearing a badly-placed, normal-sized wig.

• Suspended on wires, the two halves of a skinless woman appear to have swum through an enormous invisible saw blade - sliced wig and pubic hair nevertheless remaining dutifully attached to her either side.

• A man runs to who knows where, clutching his diseased organs in his hands - possibly trying to figure out which display case to put them in. Blanched, Plastinated organs, and sexual parts abound, sliced and diced and arranged in cabinets like flea Market ornaments.

Finally, a skinless man and skinless horse, whose corresponding body parts have been commingled for comparison, rear up together against a backdrop of flat, vertical slices of Plastinated corpse suspended on wires in the window. An artsy arrangement that takes advantage of the California sunlight to attempt a kind of new-age stain glass effect, but on account of the heat, succeeds in producing an image of warped and distorted shish kebab ingredients from hell.

Beyond the apocalyptic horseman, right before the exit through the gift shop, a TV monitor finally explains how this has all been made possible. At last the disquieting sensation assumes tangible form. Accompanied by a Kraftwerk-type soundtrack evoking the 'poignancy of man's impermanence', 'his determination to know', 'the triumph of science' etc., etc., cadavers are run through band saws, submerged in liquids, suspended in vacuum chambers, kneaded onto armatures and misted into permanence inside huge plastic tents. And at last, the maestro himself - Gunther Von Hagens - makes his appearance: a ubiquitous figure, tirelessly supervising every detail of the process: nudging an arm slightly higher, a testicle further to the left. Tipping a wig to a jauntier angle, perking a nipple to perfection. A renaissance figure in every sense of the word, the synthesis of science and art...

A man in a lab coat and black pork-pie hat.

Injecting plastic- a petroleum product - into corpses, and 'resurrecting them' is an appropriate folly for the times. Frank Zappa, who coined the term 'plastic people' is surely laughing in his grave. Regardless of the wonder of the process, it's the image of Von Hagens that leaves the most lasting impression. A beef jerky sculpture park is hardly unsettling in the obvious sense but it's not a happy place. The emotional decline while wandering through the exhibits is comparable to that experienced when watching a porno movie. The initial reaction to nakedness - which in this case has the added element of it being in the 'flesh' - is one of excitement, but the sensation quickly turns to a kind of sadness. The feeling - and knowing - that something is missing.

Studying body parts is as much an indication of the transcendent nature of their function as the disassembled components of a clock are of the idea of time. The process doesn't take us any closer to understanding, in fact it does the opposite. It generates a despair that focuses on the mortality of those being observed: our fellow human beings. The exhibits, just like the women in porno movies, are not people with that many options. Exhibiting themselves- with or without their consent - is clearly an economic expedient.

Given that over three million people in Europe have already seen the show, at presumably the same fifteen bucks a pop, it's interesting to speculate how much Von Hagens was willing to part with, for the body of a mother and unborn child. It is also worth considering whether at that price, the good doctor himself is prepared to exhibit his own remains in this way…

Skin removed, muscles twisted and flared... penis erect, hands clutching dollar bills... his signature pork-pie hat *"further narrowing the gap between life and death"*...

In the unlikely event this was to happen, what title would he choose for *himself?*

LORD OF THE BONOBOS

"... knowing just which vine to grab, and for exactly how long..."

Action novels invariably mirror the sexual dynamic. They embody the same tension/release mechanism as orgasm, and like the movies they often inspire, always result in a *climax* - in their extreme, simplistic form, with a literal explosion:

After an hour and half of mounting tension, Luke Skywalker's rocket ship finally penetrates the Deathstar and he lets go his torpedo. There is a long anticipated burst of pyrotechnics, then characters and audience alike settle back in the warm afterglow of e-mission accomplished. There is intent, a resistance to intent, a struggle to overcome it, and finally, the moment when the intent is achieved. Then there is reflection and calm. The intent can be an idea, a person, or an object that embodies an idea, but achieving it always involves *conflict*.

The Tarzan adventures of Edgar Rice Burroughs are action novels: the ongoing saga of a manly-man in the company of apes in constant conflict with the jungle, his adopted family, man-eating/ape-eating cannibals and ruthless white men bent on exploiting all three.

In the books, the future Lord Greystoke and his wife are washed ashore after a shipwreck off the west coast of Africa. A child is born, but both parents die soon after. A female ape discovers the child and convinces the rest of the tribe to let her raise it as her own. She *names* him Tarzan.

These apes are composite creatures with no actual real-world counterparts. They're not Gorillas since Gorillas are clearly established as their mortal enemies. Apart from their size (they're more than twice as big) the apes they resemble most are Chimpanzees. Their social structure is the same and as Jane Goodall confirmed in the late nineteen-sixties, they are also both meat eaters and cannibalistic - all of which adds more possibilities for conflict. They would of course be *Pan Troglodytes* Chimpanzees, not their cousins *Pan Paniscus*.

Pan Paniscus chimps or Bonobos have a very different outlook on life.

Bonobo society is predicated on *avoiding* conflict. Tension, no matter when and where it occurs, is immediately defused - through sex. As a result, Bonobo chimpanzees have some form of sex, on average, once every four and a half hours. They make no distinctions between gender or age. Young and old, male and female, indulge in manual, oral and copulatory sex whenever and with whomever they choose. They do this both to relieve anxiety *and* for enjoyment. If Tarzan had been raised by these kinds of apes, it would have been a different story altogether.

His childhood would have been essentially conflict free. His disagreements with Terchak and Tublat the dominant ape males would have been resolved with mutual masturbation or fellatio, not by terrifying fights to the death, in which scalps are torn off and hearts are ripped from rib cages. Bonobos simply don't do that sort of thing. Unlike their cousins, they don't eat meat and they certainly don't eat one another. They don't kill anything at all. For a would-be, he-man action figure this would be a serious handicap.

There would be other drawbacks too. According to Mr. Burroughs, Tarzan's older male relatives weighed in at around three hundred and fifty pounds. Given the closer relationship between body size and penis size in Bonobos – i.e. 'theirs' are relatively much bigger than 'ours', this suggests that Tarzan's childhood may have been trying at times. In keeping with the original story, it might explain why he wandered off a lot and learned to read. (*"I feel like reading tonight"* being a well-worn response to inconvenient sexual advances.)

In light of such an upbringing, Tarzan may not turn out to be quite the acrobatic hunter killer that Edgar had in mind, but what he lacked in fighting skills would be more than compensated for by an extensive repertoire of sexual strategies. A buff and horny young man, he would set off into the world fully prepared to solve each and every crisis with his johnson.

In the case of his family's mortal enemies the Mbongas, attempting to roger an entire tribe of pointy teethed cannibals into submission, would present him with far greater challenges than simply yanking them up into the trees and slitting their throats - particularly since genital manipulation by a white man, or worse yet, actually being mounted by one, would in all likelihood have only hardened their resolve. And doubly hardened it if the same tactics were also being applied to their womenfolk. Tarzan's ability to triumph over such improbable odds would require a sexual technique comparable to his remarkable ability to swing through the trees: knowing just which vine to grab, and for exactly how long, before reaching for the next.

While he was engaged in this ongoing plate spinning routine with his enemies, he would also be dealing with the confusing behavior of his so-called human friends - particularly Jane.

Bonobo meal times are occasions when fun and anxiety present themselves big time. Eating is enjoyable, but everyone is concerned they get their share. Sex and food are therefore synonymous.

When the Porter party is abandoned on the beach, food is naturally an issue, but in addition to the problems of finding it, their up-tight, English *"After you..."*, *"No, after you..."* concerns for correctness, makes them a doubly high-anxiety group; an up-tightness that only increases when table manners are involved.

Having made it his business to supply them with all they need, Tarzan would be confronted with a level of tension he's never encountered before, one that could only result in his having to patrol the table with a constant erection, ready to administer calm at the slightest hint of discomfort or distaste - or conversely - the merest sign of enjoyment. The outrage and embarrassment caused by such a no-win state of affairs would then further escalate the level of tension among the dinner guests, turning every mouthful into a potential sexual indignity.

For the castaways, food and sex would *also* become synonymous but the alternative - worrying about starving - would create apprehensions that placed them in even greater jeopardy. Esmeralda, the African maid, with her hysteria and tendency to faint at the drop of a hat, would be at particular risk. And Jane, who has the double handicap of being constantly nervous, as well as the object of Tarzan's affections, would probably spend most of her time in hiding - especially since she is also obsessed with *him*. Tarzan is a handsome, intelligent hunk of a man, and her thoughts as she buries herself in the sand each day, would be an emotional tangle of gargantuan proportion.

The classic, "*Me Tarzan. You Jane.*" line, (never uttered in the novels) would be modified to "*Me Tarzan, where Jane?*" or "*where everybody?*" for that matter. As a woman desperately in love desperately hiding from the man of her dreams, Jane would be a certifiable wreck in no time. Life in the hut, would deteriorate into a kind of Jumbo Johnny Holmes on speed meets Gilligan's Island affair, with men and women fucking and fainting left and right, only to be resuscitated by more fucking. Eventually everyone would go mad.

An essential premise of Romantic love is the notion of uniqueness, the idea that we are the sole focus of another's attention. Having your loved one suddenly slip out from behind you to cheerfully administer a blow job to your dad who's dropped his fork, then move on to diddle the befuddled maid, is difficult to reconcile in those terms, particularly when it occurs on a relentless hourly basis. Being hostage to food, nature and the intractable hard on of an overbearing wildman, could only lead to one thing:

They would have to kill him.

Despite Jane Goodall's contention that Bonobo society represents an "*Idyllic way of life*", humans can only put up with so much peace and loving. (Several women writers have swooned in print over the joys of Bonobo society, a world where love conquers all they say. But few if any of them, I venture, would trade a Bloomingdale's charge card for a lifetime of random unpredictable fucking. Where's the leverage in that?)

Bonobo life style only works for Bonobos. For other primates, even other kinds of chimpanzees, a life devoid of tension is no life at all. It doesn't *go* anywhere. This is particularly true for humans. If Tarzan had been raised by Bonobos he would have been confronted with this reality the moment he stepped out the door. His story would have contained all the requisite intents, obstacles to intents etc., but he would have been on the wrong side of the line. He would have been a sitting duck, in fact he would never have been in the picture to begin with. The pointy teethed Mbongas would have eaten all the Bonobos, long before he got there.

That's what action is all about, right Luke?

"Trust your instincts. Use the force"... Fuck the bastards.

THE GAME

"At what point in oblivion Mr. Chopra, do you propose we tee-off from..?"

Deepak Chopra runs a center for 'spiritual giddyup' in Southern California. His forte is mind-body medicine and he includes golf as a means for contemplating the essential balance between the two. In his book *Golf for Enligtenement: The Seven Lessons for the Game of Life*, he presents the "'parable" of Adam Everyman, a frustrated, hopeless golfer who achieves both superlative golfing skills and unique personal insight, thanks to Leela – a mysterious young blonde woman he meets in a shack one day after a particularly depressing round

"Life is a game," says Mr. Chopra," *and like golf, it is a game played in Eden."*

But if Life is a game, what kind of game is it, where everything plays against everything else with no perceivable outcome? A game where players come and go in relentless succession with no apparent change in the direction of play - with no idea of the rules, or the objective - a game that does not end?

A game by definition is a purposeful interaction between factions, - two people, two teams, two nations, whatever - to achieve a particular result within the context of agreed upon parameters. Everyone involved, including the spectators know what's going on. And in order to achieve its purpose, it must at some point reach a conclusion. It must have an outcome. A game of golf with an infinite number of holes cannot possibly be a game, nor a cricket match with a never-ending succession of innings - certainly not for players who live and die in the process. If the game doesn't end, what difference does the score make? Where's the incentive? What's the point?

How can a soccer player play better, if he has no idea where the goal is?

Suggesting that it is the kind of game that we play as children, amounts to the same thing. Games that children play also have intent; each child knows what the game is about, what is part of the game, and what is not. They knowingly participate in an agreed upon event, and since they are aware of the purpose, they know when they're achieving it. Even if the outcome is not to produce winners and losers, each child knows whether the game was successful or not. This is in complete contradiction to Life.

Possibly it is the kind of game involving other life forms, a more insidious range of winner loser activities including sport Fishing, Fox hunting, Pheasant shooting and Bull fighting. These are games of a sort, but they are rigged games, in that only one side knows what's going on, and as such is the only side which finds pleasure in it: A 'lesser' life-form, is unwittingly enlisted in a game of wits, where its 'natural' abilities are forced into contest against the 'intellectual' abilities of a 'superior' incomprehensible adversary. The 'lesser' life form has no concept of rules, methods, and purpose etc., but is clearly aware that failure to evade imposed circumstances will result in painful termination of sensibility. This certainly seems more analogous to the human condition - and it's painfully obvious which side we are on.

Or it could be a game of chance, a gamble, a word that shares the same etymological root. In this form of game an individual or a group of individuals proposes a configuration of future events and places objects of value in support of their conviction. Such conviction is countered by opposing points of view that are also backed in the same way. The side that predicts the correct outcome acquires the objects of the opposition. The possibilities for this form of game are almost limitless since reality is always in flux. Everything is subject to outcome - the roll of a dice, the turn of a card, the spin of a wheel, the weather, the war, the weight of a baby. But if Life is a gamble, it's not Life that's making the wager, Life *is* the wager or simply the event that's being wagered against. Either it is the currency or the ball in the wheel, a mere cipher in the hands of an indifferent sensibility.

As with the other forms of game it fails as an analogy simply because Life in order to play, must know what it is playing *for*. Without that, it cannot know whether it is winning or losing, and without that, it is denied the one essential purpose of all games: the joy of knowing that it has played well. In its despair, it cannot even walk off the field, since the field is without boundaries.

Which brings us to Eden.

The coupling of Eden and innocence is invariably accepted without question, innocence being a state of existence, free from moral wrong. In its childhood as it were, without the guile and duplicity that characterizes its maturity. Eden we are told was paradise, a perfect place; it was harmony, wellbeing, bliss.

But if nothing went wrong in Eden, then nothing could go right there either. It would be bound by its perfection. There couldn't even *be* a there because without relativistic consciousness there would be no sense of *here* to compare it to. It wouldn't be a *place* at all, it would be nowhere, nothing, oblivion. Not the innocence of childhood, but the moment before the child is conceived.

At what point in oblivion Mr. Chopra, do you propose we tee-off from?

By suggesting that golf can be played in Eden, Deepak Chopra simply evokes the same old, fairytale, never-never land from children's books. A place invented in Genesis and epitomized by the Watchtower illustrations of the Jehovah's Witnesses: implausible tableaus in which black-folks and white-folks (in clothes that do somewhat resemble golf outfits) pose together amongst carnivores and herbivores alike, gazing out over backdrops of lush mountains and perfect sky. Images that prompt any thinking person over the age of five to ask, "*And what happens when it gets dark?*" When he describes the golf course as such a perfect garden, Chopra can only be referring to the photographs in the Club brochures, which like the illustrations of the Jehovah's witnesses, advertise an idyllic freeze frame of unreality, well worth the price of admission.

Golf is above all a game of privilege, and in that sense the Biblical image of Eden *is* appropriate. It is played by a small cross section of life in ideal surroundings often in stark contrast to what exists beyond them. Until recently, it has always been a white man's game, like polo, or fox hunting or elephant safaris. It is an appropriate irony that a young man named Tiger Woods emerged to redefine the idea. Cost alone makes it inaccessible to the majority of people. A typical golf course consumes the amount of water used by a town of thirty thousand people. It covers an average area of 150 plus acres. Maintenance costs are enormous. Membership fees reflect these parameters. It is a game often associated with weekends, and as such, the slew of books equating the game with a form of spiritual communion presumably justifies hundreds of thousands of would be/ should be, church goers, into coming to peace with their abscondance.

Most significantly it is an insulated reality: the hoi poloi cannot intrude on its manicured perfection. Homeless people won't stray here or any of the country's undernourished. They don't even exist here. Chopra hints at this idea momentarily in his fable of Adam Everyman: while anticipating his next golf lesson, Adam refers to an image on television, of a war somewhere *"far away"* which he immediately switches off.

It is in that sentence, that Mr. Chopra gives the game away.

Golf like most games, is a device for switching *off* reality, both for players and audience alike. It narrows our focus down to a small white ball. And we do this precisely because Life is not a game. It is a relentless onslaught where only a few are able to avoid suffering. Golf isn't played by the people of Rwanda or Palestine or Iraq, it is played by the kind of people who help create such worlds.

Are these the people the parable of Adam Everyman and Leela appeals to? A male whack-off/tee-off fantasy, about a fabulous blonde girl hooker/slicer who lures a middle aged man into a lonely shack in the middle of nowhere? A pretty girl in shorts and a pony tail patiently kneading his corrosive doubts into conviction; improving his strokes, adjusting his woods, coaxing his balls toward the hole. *"Not rimming it, but driving to its center."* Oi! Is this the fantasy that appeals to the privileged? The movers and shakers?

The ex-president of the United States and his father are golfers, and when asked what he and his father talk about when they're not talking politics, George W. replied:

"Pussy"

Not the existential nature of the game?

Please. They're out there to get away from the wife and kids, probably get drunk and while they're at it, figure out which unwitting sons of bitches they're going to drop a bomb on.

Mr. Chopra does not advocate such ideas of course, his solution to the Iraq situation in 2003 was that the country should be disarmed without force. He gave no indication of how this would be achieved but suggested that a Disneyland theme park might help, along with free access to MTV, Nickelodeon and CNN. Maybe a couple of golf courses wouldn't hurt either.

And so it goes...

Having paid the exorbitant fee, the golfer steps to the green. He tees his first shot and the moment the club hits the ball the game begins. The dice are rolled. The 'PAIR O' DICE' – Adam and Eve. In that moment, the notion of Eden disappears. Game cannot be played there, game is what destroys it. Game is duality, male and female, good and evil, life and death. It is winners and losers, and inevitably, it is suffering. The moment the ball begins to move, the stuff of life sets in: apprehension, doubt, envy, fear, and failure. We are forced to decide, forced to define ourselves, with no sense of purpose or outcome or reason.

While beyond the *fair*way, in the *roughs* of all eternity, a billion hapless souls, murder and consume one another forever.

If we must resort to the same old Biblical metaphors...

The game of golf is not played in Eden Mr. Chopra – like life, it is played in Hell.

INTENTION

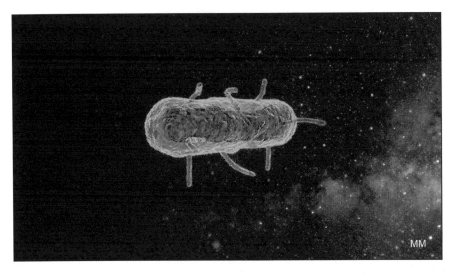

"A human 'being' is conscious of itself *long* before it thinks. ..."

The armies of *Yersinia pestis* destroyed more than *fifty million* human beings during the fourteenth century alone - more than the combined hordes of Genghis Khan and Attila the Hun many times over. Like them, they also came from the East. How many more were massacred on the way is unknowable. Two thirds of the population of Europe would succumb to their ravages during that century, and as they had done for centuries before, human beings would continue to die on a massive scale for centuries to come.

Yersinia pestis is the bacterium of Plague, a microscopic, ultra-efficient adversary that waits; biding its time, sending out sorties, waiting on chance. It is a parasite, a life form that co-opts the energies of another. It *knows* to do this. It also *knows* it must recruit an intermediary, to gain access to the organism it needs. This is *strategy*: a deliberately contrived sequence of actions to affect a specific outcome; an awareness of *intention* evinced by a life form all but invisible to us.

A Flea is also a parasite - a bloodsucker - for *Yersinia pestis*, the perfect assault vehicle and Trojan horse. By infiltrating and blocking the flea's digestive tract, the bacteria make it impossible for it to feed without regurgitating its meal back into the host. The Reflux of one organism thereby becomes the bridgehead for invasion by a second - into the blood stream of a third. In the fourteenth century, that third happened to be Marmots - the Groundhogs of Mongolia.

Marmots would not be the cause of Plague per se, fleas aren't picky, one mammal, one rodent, is as good as another. Rats are a particular favorite since they are so ubiquitous. Rats, have latched onto the biggest, most successful parasite of them all, a mammal riding upon the back of another that has spread its own version of *intention* to every corner of the earth.

If not for the forced symbiosis, i.e. parasitism, of ape upon horse, human Culture would not exist as we know it. Conceivably, since they first encountered them, humans have overpowered horses and put them to work: agriculture, transportation, exploration and conquest would not have happened without them. The worldwide spread of Culture, therefore, like the worldwide spread of Plague is also the effect of one life form appropriating another to its own ends. Culture has arguably destroyed a greater diversity of planetary organisms than all the other forms of parasitism combined. Does it constitute a disease?

The China Silk Road, commandeered by the militaristic horse culture of the Khans, provided the perfect on-ramp for *Yersinia pestis* from Asia into Europe. It wouldn't be the first time: Justinian's Plague in the fifth century wiped out twenty-five to fifty million, men, women and children over time, and it was also 'Made In China'. In each case, when the path ran out, everyone climbed onto ships - humans, horses, rats, fleas, and *Yersinia* - one big happy family; a traveling Petri dish in which Culture was literally the medium.

A human being is a formidable emplacement; a hive of mutually dependent intentions determined to resist at all cost, anything and everything that would attempt to undermine it. But it is no match for Plague. Plague is an invasion force whose victory is almost assured. It has never been here before, but it *knows* what to do. It swarms into the labyrinth of ducts, *knowing* how to avoid macrophages, the body's defensive cells, *knowing* how to defuse the waves of phagocytes and amoebic protozoans marshaled against it. It *knows* how to jam the signaling of the cytokine defenses, and *knows* how to seek out the Lymph nodes. Once there, it *knows* it has won. It has realized the high ground of *intention*.

Its objective secured, Plague will proliferate exponentially, doubling its population every one and a half hours. In a week or so, it will have established an incontestable empire of billions. Eventually, however, it will deplete the environment that sustains it. Colony and colonizers will collapse irrevocably.

Life feeds on life, and we are no exception. *Homo sapiens* even colonize themselves in the same ongoing process of increase and dissolution. It is a process informed by the most profound sense of knowing, an awareness *outside* of time, *ahead* of time, that organizes matter into 'being' *within* it. It is the anticipation of future that propels the sperm to its objective and compels the egg to move to meet it. A human 'being' is conscious of itself *long* before it thinks. It is the awareness of *intention* that compels us to *speak*.

Language is the basis of Culture, and Culture is the strategy by which human beings colonize and increase. Like the strategy of Plague it must also adapt to circumstances that are never the same. In that regard we are surely equal. We may think that language - the means for articulating that idea – makes us somehow superior, but when confronted by *Yersinia pestis* we are invariably contradicted.

Culture spread to North America in the 1500s but it took Plague another four hundred years to catch up. Setting out from China once again, it swept through India and Pakistan in 1896, killing over twelve million, and from there took ship to Hawaii killing a few more. In 1900 it arrived in San Francisco where - for the sake of appearances - the governor declared it a 'safe city' and cancelled the quarantine of the Chinatown district where the outbreak had occurred. Over a hundred died as a result. It was finally sent packing when the great earthquake fire of 1906, swept the city and 'conveniently' burned Chinatown to the ground. Twenty years later it showed up in Los Angeles.

Yersinia pestis is still reported in the United States, and California is still a popular hide out, along with Colorado, New Mexico and

Arizona. California ground squirrels, and prairie dogs are prominent vectors and campgrounds were closed on their account as recently as 2015.

Yersinia pestis also likes cats: Housecats. Cats harboring plague can infect people through bites, scratches, coughs, or sneezes – and of course - fleas. A cat flea jumps an average horizontal distance of eight inches, and an average height of five inches. With the best *intention*, it can jump as far as nineteen inches and as a high as eight.

"Here kitty kitty."

ANT WEATHER

"…many, *many* Cocker Spaniels will die…"

In New York City, the insects I encountered most frequently were cockroaches. In L.A. it was ants. My respect for each is naturally profound, but it differs according to their specific forms of social organization - their sense of community as it were and their response to the hazards with which they have to contend.

Cockroaches display a far greater sense of individualism. When confronted by a threat, they evidence a measured consideration of possible response and outcome: which way to run, whether to run at all etc. Ants on the other hand tend to move without pause in all directions at once. It's a distinction that becomes especially apparent when they're assaulted by their own versions of weather.

Cockroaches and ants have both latched onto the human urban life style; understandably, both are to be found where the food is at. When they're discovered by their human benefactors, helping themselves to it, they're invariably subject to incomprehensibly intractable forces of destruction that even an insectoid Albert E. would be at a loss to explain.

In order to get a sense of the realities they encounter, it is necessary to consider scale:

If an ant crawls onto our arm we invariably flick it off without a moment's pause. Picturing the victim in terms of a small dog however, with purpose, sense of self, sense of danger, sense of mortality and so on slows this knee jerk response significantly. If we imagine we've smeared out a Cocker Spaniel or a Chihuahua in such a cold dismissive way, the idea gets a little harder to reconcile. If we then place ourselves alongside the event in our normal dog to human size relationship, the instant, unpredictable carnage is almost impossible to contemplate - especially if the scenario involves hundreds of Cocker Spaniels at once.

Ants are approximately one thousand times smaller than we are. A kitchen sink therefore, which is a good place to witness ant weather, is the human geographical equivalent of a six hundred and sixty foot deep canyon. The ants nevertheless run up and down these sheer walls at around twenty-five miles an hour, a speed they maintain almost consistently. Given that the rim of the sink is probably thirty-six inches from ground level, they have already run three thousand vertical feet to get there. They're there at all on account of wide ranging individual scouts who discovered the food, then conveyed its location via a complex system of communication relays. The result was a column of hundreds running back and forth within minutes, most of which had left from a home base sometimes as much as five to ten ant-miles distant - also covered at the same relentless speed.

Unlike normal climactic vicissitudes, to which all life forms are subject, ant weather rains down from a clear sky with specific deadly precision. It is a sudden, implacable, aerial bombardment with *their* name on it, and on account of it, many, *many* Cocker Spaniels will die.

Setting a coffee cup down on the counter in order to ponder its options, a human being creates an event equivalent to a three hundred and fifty foot diameter, thousand pound flat rock suddenly and unpredictably pounding to earth out of nowhere at about sixty miles an hour. Such a sudden eruption of geographical violence is impossible to strategize against. For those not actually pulverized by it, the sound and concussion results in an overwhelming sense of disorientation. Running without pause in all directions at once, is the only possible result. An equal number of Harvard PhDs, or Mensa folks on a picnic would exhibit the same behavior.

For those actually in the sink, the human response is simple: the faucet instantly takes care of the food source and countless hapless hungry diners along with it. There are no Noah ants in this scenario. Destruction is total.

After deluge comes sponge: a seven hundred square foot, water soaked aerial bulldozer, ramming down with the force of many thousand foot-pounds, pushing and smearing hundreds around the rim of the canyon and back along the line of entry into a soggy pile of limbs and mangled torsos. And following sponge, paper towel: "*Sweeping down the plain, right behind the rain*", gathering up the dead, half dead and living alike and crushing them to a paste.

The column nevertheless continues to emerge from the crack in the countertop. There is clearly confusion among its ranks and its pace has slowed. This operation may have been underway for hours, functioning flawlessly back and forth, but now the forward contingent has unaccountably disappeared without trace. And as more unsuspecting individuals stumble out into the light, the yellow peril descends over and again to obliterate them. Feedback is impossible under such conditions, victims just keep stumbling into oblivion.

Having stemmed the tide, the weather now moves to stop the flow altogether.

"Ant Chalk" is sold only in Chinatown. The warning label reads: "*Keep away from children and the old man.*" Whether this implies that ant killing is a wife's prerogative or simply only for the sturdy and mature is unclear, but stuff that's risky to humans is most assuredly deadly to something one-thousandth their size. A line drawn with Ant Chalk is an impenetrable toxic barrier that will leave hundreds dead on either side of it: a surreal white avalanche of greasy powder that descends from above to delineate a path that chokes to death within minutes all ants that come close. Just enough time, however, for those contaminated, to spread the poison back along the line.

The point of entry is thus secured. All that remains of the weather is one last flurry of paper to tidy up the aftermath, then all is calm. Hundreds of busy life forms have disappeared without trace; order is restored.

The instrument of weather sits back with its coffee, a job well done. So much for ants it thinks – if it thinks about them at all. Insect automatons, robot workers, in an itty-bitty totalitarian world, mindlessly going about their allotted tasks, eating for no other reason than to make more ants. They act the same, they look the same, they're not like us at all. It is questionable though whether as many miniaturized naked Frenchmen scrambling around on all fours would suggest more individual personality. Electron scanning microscopy in fact reveals differences in ant physiognomy that belies the idea of sameness entirely. They are as different looking as we are.

The matter however is moot. Regardless of individual distinction it is their significance as a group that points up the irony: the fact is, they are actually *bigger* than we are. Pound for planetary pound they outweigh us. The ants of the world weigh *four times* as much as the reptiles, amphibians, mammals and birds combined. In the South Eastern United States alone there are an estimated 2.5 billion *tons* of fire ants. E.O. Wilson calculated that the ant biomass in a rain forest is 10% of its total weight.

As much as we may dismiss them, we cannot do without them. *They* are the clean up squad, the movers and enrichers of the earth. If ants disappeared from the planet, humans would most likely follow soon after. If humans disappeared, ants would hardly blink. In which event, tomorrow's ant weather forecast might read:

"Beginning cloudy, later sunny, no chance of sponge."

NOAH

"And 10,000 snakes slither away laughing..."

As most children will tell you, one human being alone is responsible for the remarkable abundance of fauna that inhabits the planet. According to the Biblical Genesis, it was Noah, the kindly old gent of antiquity, who almost single handedly achieved what is unquestionably the most spectacular ecological event of all time.

Noah of course, like all Biblical dignitaries, was merely following orders. It was *God* who had decided to drown all living forms and *God* who had devised the convoluted strategy for nevertheless saving representative specimens of each.

The story of Noah therefore, really concerns the nature of this God, a God who despairs over the human beings He has created and decides to destroy all but a few of them. As many children will also tell you, it is a bad workman who blames his tools. So what kind of workman is it, then, who blames the tools He has made *Himself*... and made in His *own image?*

Chapter five of Genesis is devoted to a genealogical catalogue of the begettings from Adam to Noah, in the course of which, many daughters are necessarily born into the world. Chapter six begins:

> 1. And it came to pass that men began to multiply on the earth, and daughters were born unto them.
> 2. That the sons of God saw the daughters of men that they were fair; and they took them wives of all that they saw...
> 4. There were giants in the earth in those days; and also after that, when the sons of God came in unto the daughters of men, and they bare children to them, the same became mighty men of renown,

Much has been made of this reference to "giants" yet what it refers *to* is typically unclear. Having briefly alluded to them, our reporter moves abruptly along to describe how God's sons had been cavorting with the local girls and how popular their offspring had become in the neighborhood. There is a vague implication that it is *they* who were giant, but this would have created obvious sexual complications. It would also have placed God's punishing routine beyond the pale. He has already unfairly sentenced women to painful childbirth and now He has allowed his sons to impregnate them with enormous children. We must assume therefore that their mightiness was of an intellectual nature. They were of human stature, with sexual proclivities to match.

(I was under the impression Christianity was FOUNDED on the idea that God – this *same* God – so loved the world that He "gave

His ONLY begotten son" as its redeemer. That being the case, where do this lot fit in?)

Whatever the nature of these other sons of God may be, the fact that they are subject to the same kinds of sexual urges as hyenas and muskrats and apparently comfortable with the idea of 'settling down', makes them remarkably ungodlike. Conceivably there are no women of their own stature where they come from – and they must come from somewhere, since conventional fatherhood, suggests conventional space/time orientation and makes them subject to place. In their defense, having a father who is omnipresent does make home life a little cramped. This might account for why there is no mention of their mother. With God being everywhere there is simply nowhere to put her. How she produced sons is a conundrum of Einsteinian proportion.

Regardless of their home life, their father not only condones their behavior toward earthly women, but He even betrays a certain grandfatherly pride for their offspring – in verse four that is. In verse five, immediately after His family has entered the picture, God decides that things have gone seriously wrong.

> 5. And God saw that the wickedness of man was great in the earth, and that every imagination of the thoughts of his heart was only evil continually.

Apparently, what His mighty grandchildren were renown for was wickedness – or at least they contributed to it – which they can only have inherited from their fathers and which they in turn can only have inherited from their father – God.

Who now has a problem, a problem that will confront countless earthly tyrants, despots and political crooks to come, who find themselves exposed behind the curtain. One that has but a single simple blatant solution:

Destroy the evidence and blame someone else.

Having blamed His own creative shortcomings on Adam and Eve, He places the responsibility for His family's unruly behavior on the entire human race – and just to be on the safe side – everything else as well.

> GEN. 6: v.7 And the Lord said, I will destroy man whom I have created from the face of the earth; both man, and beast, and the creeping thing, and the fowls of the air; for it repenteth me that I have made them.

He will drown them all, guilty and innocent alike, right down to the unborn children. Only one man and his family will be saved, along with representatives of each of the life forms that now infest the planet.

Six hundred year-old Noah, whom one would think had already had more than his share of living, pops up out of nowhere to do the job; similar to the way presidential candidates do, with no indication of their particular virtues. In a part of the world notable for its sparseness of vegetation, he is instructed to build an enormous wooden boat, the technical and practical impossibilities of which are far too numerous to mention. The significant fact is, that when the rains come, anyone not on the boat will die. Which prompts the question, what happens to God's own grandchildren? Were they to be airlifted out at the last minute, Saigon style, or will God drown them along with everyone else? To top off His contradictory, arbitrary, forgetful, bullying, deceitful personality, does He now murder His own family? It's a Prozac nightmare. What kind of heavenly Father is this? More importantly, is this the image after which *we* were created?

This motherless God of the Bible clearly has little respect for womankind. It was Eve who was blamed for His initial shortcomings and now the daughters of men who are to be unfairly punished for the behavior of His sons. Just like the snake they will get off scot-free. If a snake had indeed been responsible for the derailing of His perfect world, it seems now would be the perfect opportunity to be rid of such reprehensible creatures once and for all. Instead, He allows two of each species onto the boat. Given that the order *Ophidae* contains some 5,000 members, that's a total of 10,000 vipers, rattlesnakes, mambas, boa constrictors etc., in all.

Being omniscient means a knowledge of all things - those that *are*, those that *were*, and those that *will be*. In that respect the God of the Old Testament does on occasions exhibit proof of such talent. As well as forgetting that some things have *already* happened, however, there are times when He clearly forgets that so far they *haven't*. His instructions regarding "clean" and "unclean" can only have appeared to Noah as nonsense compounding folly.

The definition of these terms will only become apparent to the world, when God Himself reveals it for the *first* time to Moses – a few hundred years in the future – yet Noah has to somehow figure it out for himself in no time quick. In the context of a world about to be completely flooded, the cleanest of creatures one might assume would be those in the water, but in this matter alone Noah reveals his suitability for the job. Not only can he build a mile long boat in a desert and summon representatives of all the world's creatures to climb aboard it, but he's able to assign seating arrangements based on God-given, futuristic, instructional gibberish.

With clean and unclean alike, safe and sound in the floating madhouse, the deluge goes ahead on schedule, and our heavenly father establishes once and for all, his obscenely violent, arbitrary, bullying nature, and imperviousness to the suffering of the souls He has invested.

Seven months and seven days later, the water abates and the boat comes to rest on a mountain of mud and dead children named Ararat. Four months after that, the improbable zoo finally disembarks, and two by two, sets off for the four corners of the flat circular earth to be fruitful and multiply – yet again. And we're back to square one.

Almost.

In the course of all this slaughter, God has apparently reached several conclusions – one would hope as a result of seeing all those desperate bubbles rising to the surface, but not so. They occur to him in the course of yet more carnage.

Despite the fact that He has just drowned countless, caring, loving, innocent souls, He now insists for a finale that Noah select *"of every clean beast and of every clean fowl"* and offer burnt offerings on the altar! Imagine: after seven months of being cooped up on a boat to avoid being drowned, you finally step out into the fresh air and get set on fire.

> GEN.8: v20. And the Lord smelled a sweet savor; and the Lord said in his heart, I will not again curse the ground any more for man's sake; for the imagination of man's heart is evil from his youth; neither will I again smite any more every living thing, as I have done.

The smell of burning flesh inspires Him to admit once and for all, that people – whom He has created – are just no darn good. Punishing them is a waste of time. Never again will He go to all that trouble. Unlike a car manufacturer who owns up to faulty steering and recalls his product for modification, God simply shakes His head and says *"Whaddya gonna do?"* He gives up. Rather than try to fix them - which he should be able to do, He is God after all – He leaves them the way they are.

Not only has He once again demonstrated all too human fallibility by doing something then admitting it was wrong, but He now adds a kind of lazy defeatism to His modus operandi. As if the real reason for all that water was simply to wash His hands of His own responsibilities. Everything else was secondary, an insight that only occurs to Him as thousands and thousands more unwitting life forms go up in smoke – learning the true meaning of "cleanliness is next to Godliness."

And 10,000 snakes slither away laughing.

Hard to believe – right kids?

PIGGY IN THE MIDDLE

"In which scheme of things, we are merely the fuel… "

Every dogma has its day and every generation sets another flawless category among the pigeonholes: a flat earth, an earth supported by elephants, an earth around which the entire universe revolves even. *Geo*centrism was the name of that one, a trusty old dog only recently put down. We smile now, the way we always do, when we've buried another essential truth. Sun around the earth? how impossibly naïve!

Yet Centrism's pedigree perseveres. Six hundred years on, *Homo*centrism insists that regardless of the comings and goings of the universe, everything still revolves around *us*. Human beings that is, nature's supreme achievement; a wonderful Biblical/Darwinian conceit that relegates every other life form on Earth to mere backdrop - something to pose next to for scale as it were. Then there is *Ethno*centrism, the finer distinction that proposes one category of Homos is more important than the rest. Chosen that is. Or Blessed. Or Exalted. A piggy in the middle conviction based on which group has the best imaginary friend.

This pivotal pigginess is not a static condition. It is subject to another remarkable conceit called *progress*: the idea that we are *going* somewhere. The question of course is where? After all, where are elephants going? Where is the weather going? Where are the trees outside the window going? Tree-ness is a constant, weather-ness is a constant, so why not Human-ness? We're no smarter now than we ever were. We don't love more, hate more, nor strive to improve our lot more. All that changes is the means by which we do it: the tools.

That tools are going somewhere can possibly be argued. Unlike us they do appear to be improving. In our folly, however, we appropriate that improvement as our own. Tools we say are the clearest evidence that it is *us* alone that are doing the going. Ultimately we will use them to leave the planet.

But these tools and machines and the computer brains that control them, are constructed from rock. Rock that we 'same' humans have been *compelled* to configure and reconfigure over millions of years. It's rock, not us, that's going somewhere. If anything is figuring out how to leave the planet, it's the planet. In which scheme of things, we are merely the fuel.

Being the means to an end does not sit well with Homos. It flies in the face of their most cherished conceit of all: *Freewill*: the conviction that they are in control of their actions.

A bizarre idea.

A man born with one leg must necessarily hop. The one follows inevitably upon the other; as in all behavior, each man forced to act according to the restraints specific to his own condition. What he does, being the result of what he came in *with*, reacting to what he came in *to*. He has no control over either - including the need to convince himself that he does. This is not a complex metaphysical issue, it's simple math, ask any third grader.

When multiplying numbers, no matter how big they are, or how many, if just one zero is included in the equation, the answer is always zero. If there is just one aspect of man's behavior therefore over which he has zero control then no matter what follows the result is zero.

Man has no control over the moment he's conceived, the moment he's born, the environment he's born into, the family he's born into, the racial type, religious type, geographical location, and historical context. He has no control over the fact that he is even a human being.

Zero.

So why is he compelled to think otherwise? Why does he insist on the further restraints of a self-imposed fiction?

Because he HAS NO CHOICE.

Because without freewill, there can be no accountability, without accountability there can be no punishment and without punishment there can be no deterrent to mayhem.

Every dogma *will* have its day and those who do not conform to it *must* be brought to heel - burned, hanged, tortured, raped, bombed, whatever. If they weren't, it would be a complete fucking madhouse down here.

VECTOR

"…prompted almost certainly by the feeling it was destined to be…"

On July 28ᵗʰ 1945, at 9.49 am, a plane crashed into the 79ᵗʰ floor of the Empire State Building - at that time, the tallest building in New York. On September 11, 2001, at 9.03 am, a plane crashed into the 79ᵗʰ floor of the South Tower of the World Trade Center – also the tallest building in the city at the time.

Among those trapped in the Empire State Building was a nineteen year-old secretary named Therese Willig. *"The first time I went in there."* said Therese *"I was all agog because here were these little wisps of clouds drifting in the window"* In those days there was no air conditioning in the building and the windows could be opened. Now, clouds of flame and smoke swept through her office, and she watched in horror, as co-worker "Mr. Fountain" staggered across the floor on fire from head to foot. In a gesture of despair, she removed the rings from her fingers and threw them out the window.*" I won't be around to have them I thought - someone else might as well have use out of them"*

One engine of the plane smashed through the building and out the far side, the other plummeted down the elevator shaft. 11 office workers were killed, but Therese, although injured, survived, and... rooting through the rubble on 34th Street below... a fireman miraculously found her rings and returned them.

One of the rings had been given to her by her boyfriend, and later she would marry him - a decision prompted almost certainly by the feeling it was destined to be. In time they would have a son named George... and in 1977, when he was 27 years old ... George, would be the first and only person to climb the South Tower of the World Trade Center.

They called him the Human Fly... fly as in VECTOR:

a) an organism esp. an insect that transmits a pathogen.
b) a force or influence .
c) a guide to an aircraft in flight.

"There are more things in heaven and earth..."

CLIMATE

"Correctness has always been big on fire…"

One hundred and ninety-nine years ago in June, snow fell on Albany New York. Six months earlier, Central Italy experienced the worst snowstorms on record. The snow was red and yellow.

Between the end of 1815 and the summer of 1816 the weather in Western Europe and North Eastern America oscillated between heat and extreme cold. Continuous rain in Europe and frosts and snow in America reduced both sides of the Atlantic to agricultural wastelands. By the end of 1816, thousands were starving.

In April 1815, Napoleon Bonaparte had been on the lam for three months and was back in Paris to pick up where he had left off. Hundreds of thousands of men and boys had died thus far promoting his version of political correctness, now he would militarize the country once again to finish the job. Two months later he was finally confronted by the British, Prussian and Belgian forces at aptly named Waterloo. Unusually intense rain for two days straight had turned the battlefield into a quagmire and the conflict - that historians suggest may otherwise have gone in Napoleon's favor - found him instead, up to his ass in mud, defeated and stuck back in jail once and for all. Weather – and Wellington boots - had combined to defeat one of history's more prolific consumers of human beings.

After decades of conflict, Europe was finally opened up for tourism again. By 1816, The Grand Tour was in full swing, with the British well-to-do and hippies of their day, able at last to indulge their finer tastes for history and culture. By now, the rain was almost a permanent condition: day after day, month after month and when it wasn't raining there was incongruous ice and snow – sometimes in reds and yellows and flesh colors. Tourism was awash. Boats floated over the tops of bridges and crops rotted under water. In an attempt to at least feed their livestock, farmers rowed out to try and harvest the fodder.

Confined to their house on the edge of Lake Geneva, the touring Shelleys and their friend Lord Byron spent the downpour reading together and inventing stories - in keeping with conditions outside - ghost stories and tales of gloom and horror. They competed with each other to invent ones of their own and out of the thunder and lightning came Frankenstein, Mary Shelley's towering metaphysical masterpiece: a book written by an 18 year-old that would give life to a truly novel, enduring fictional genre.

Back home in England, fellow 'Romantic' Joseph Turner, "*The Painter of Light*", was also confronting the weather. Pink, orange and yellow skies began to appear in his images, reflecting the actual skies above. Burning sunsets, blanketing rain and columns of steam and cloud now characterized his landscapes, raising his art to a level of elemental abstraction that would transform landscape painting - all painting - forever.

Across the Atlantic, the Eastern United States struggled with its own climactic mayhem: not a surfeit of water, but a lack of it: one month of drought followed another. There was snow in June and September in New York and Massachusetts, with oscillating extremes of heat and cold in between. It was described as the "*Year Without Summer*" and just as they had in Europe, crops and harvest were devastated and thousands faced famine.

Eighty percent of Americans depended on the crops and food they produced and in the face of ultimate disaster, thousands moved west to find better prospects. Europeans in turn immigrated to America and joined the exodus. There was plenty of room: to fund his planned invasion of England, Napoleon had doubled the size of the United States by agreeing to the Louisiana Purchase. Investors and speculators quickly handed out money to encourage relocation and just as it would in the twenty first century, risky lending and desperate borrowing in the context of economic uncertainty led to the foreclosing of mortgages, recalling of loans and collapse of banks. In 1819, the US experienced the first financial crash in its history.

Among those swept up in the chaos was a young Frenchman, whose father had hustled him out of France to save him from military impressment. If not for Napoleon's insatiable appetite for cannon fodder, America might never have heard of him.

John James Audubon had painted nature since he was a teenager and when he arrived in the new world, he determined to produce the definitive record of its birdlife. With a new family to support, he tried small business ventures selling 'dry goods' and supplies to the migrating pioneers to help fund his project, but the economic vicissitudes ultimately left him penniless. Eventually he found work aboard flatboats doing the very thing he did best: shoot birds ... and paint them. At a time when Americans ate just about anything that moved, he supplied food for the passengers by hunting the wildlife up and down the riverbanks from Pittsburg to the (now American) city of New Orleans... and increased his portfolio in the process. Two years later he was in England with a publisher and the rest is history. A French draft dodger, swept along by the tumultuous currents of circumstance, had raised the bar for wildlife painting to a height no one would surpass.

The cause of the climactic upheaval was a single event - like Napoleon Bonaparte, a violent, unpredictable force of energy that had erupted into the world without warning. Mt. Tambora, an obscure volcano, on a remote island, in faraway Indonesia had exploded with greater force than any that preceded it. Spewing ash and chemicals into the stratosphere, it had enveloped the planet in an aerosol cloud of sulphuric acid that reflected back sunlight and plunged the surface into a gloom of fogs, rains and freezing temperatures. The rainy seasons in India and China were also disrupted, leading to crop failures, flooding and starvation. As it had in Europe, disease followed in the wake of hunger with Cholera and Typhus killing many more. A single unpredictable climactic event caused social, political and economic upheaval that would be felt for decades.

The causal links between these events is incontestable but the connections involve improbable convolutions of circumstance that were far too discreet to be predicted. These in turn were the result of the unforeseeable sequence of causes and effects that had preceded them. A *"whiff of grapeshot"* had launched Napoleon's career and it had resulted in the United States doubling in size; from that came Manifest Destiny and America's position in the world today. Mary Shelley's book changed the perception of women's creative power and Audubon's cataloguing of American wildlife inspired environmental and ecological awareness; singular events that changed *everything* in effect, each – in that instance - contingent upon a singular unpredictable change in climate.

Weather, like war, compels the technological dynamic and increases our cognitive range of self. Neither is predictable with respect to its moments of origin, duration, magnitude of destruction or subsequent effects. Neither is there a measurable, quantitative correlation between the adverse and *beneficial* nature of those effects. Constant unpredictable change is the intractable condition of life. *"Change"*, the wonderfully vacuous and redundant slogan of past years seems in line with that idea – except when it comes to the weather.

The outrageous sunsets of Los Angeles are said to be caused by the vast number of Hollywood producers, actors and actresses blowing hot air up each other's asses all day. A similar idea may account for forest fires, hurricanes and disappearing polar bears: an equally large number of climate alarmists and social activists appears to be doing the same thing. The reason for their alarm (understandably) is that the air is apparently getting hotter.

The implications of this, we are told, are melting ice caps, rising sea levels, increased ocean acidity, inundation of cities, loss of wildlife, destruction of the environment and conceivably the end of civilization as we know it... but it can be averted. Carbon emissions - primarily from the burning of fossil fuels - are the reason for this apocalyptic certainty, and a halt to the process will return us to sanity and rescue us from the brink of disaster.

These conclusions have not been arrived at through the normal processes of science: the dialectic of thesis, antithesis and synthesis has been overridden. '*Thesis*' has been disproportionately funded and promoted, while contrary viewpoints have been dismissed and vilified, its proponents even being expelled from the process of research altogether. Without the equal consideration of alternatives, no reasonable synthesis is possible.

Modern computer technology can amass volumes of statistics, but given that the theoretical models of the "97% of Climate scientists" cannot present an unequivocal consensus of *what has already happened in the past*, claims for predicting effects decades into the future are questionable to say the least. Wars can also be reduced to statistics, but predicting the details of future wars based on theoretical models would be preposterous. To then propose a Correct means for countering these hypothetical effects is doubly questionable - particularly since this same Climate Science states categorically that they *cannot* be questioned.

We are dependent on oil. In addition to fuelling the private jets of celebrities traveling the world to denounce it, it is used for just about every other item in the home. A barrel of 42 gallons produces slightly less than 20 gallons of gasoline, the rest is required for such things as −aspirin, toothpaste, antiseptics, hair dyes, nail polish, perfumes, contact lenses, vitamin capsules, pantyhose, shower curtains, heart valves, deodorant, lipstick, shoes, crayons, balloons, sunglasses, toilet seats, and guitar strings - to name but a very few. An alternative source for producing most of these items has not yet been found, nor the means for transporting them. Airplanes, trucks and cargo ships cannot be powered by windmills. Neither can school buses or ambulances. Apparently a system has to be devised whereby oil is *rationed*, allowing only for essential purposes. The question then becomes, who decides what is essential? And to whom?

A worldwide banning of fossil fuel energy (which has nothing to do with fossils) increases the cost of energy, particularly for developing countries that are prevented from using their own resources for their own needs. They must struggle instead with expensive, less efficient methods dictated by the 'superior insight' of those who rose to their own levels of comfort and prosperity through precisely the means they are preventing them from using. For all their pretensions of 'sharing the wealth' they would not have other cultures share their own.

'Banning' is the corner stone of Correctness. It is not about cause and effect but fault and accountability, a non-scientific, quasi-religious viewpoint that blames the capricious unruliness of circumstance on the behavior of other human beings. In this scenario, every idea perceived as contrary must be confronted and removed – if necessary, by force. Correctness has always been big on fire: Setting fire to books, setting fire to people, setting fire to flags, setting fire to colleges - and having scientists, professors and writers with opposing points of view summarily... *fired*. In light of that, the fear that others may ostensibly be trying to set fire to *them* makes perfect sense.

Heat is not a constant tone but a series of oscillating, unequal peaks and valleys, encapsulated in turn within greater configurations. The dialogue between Earth and Sun is a 4-billion year-old intimacy impervious and indifferent to human striving: two vast incomprehensible entities communicating in a language of energies too subtle and complex to formulate, much less predict in its consequences. It was ongoing long before we got here, it will continue long after we are gone.

Climate Science and the idea that a Correct method can be discerned for determining 'change for the better' is not about controlling weather but controlling people. It is part of a globalist agenda posing as universal free thought that seeks to eradicate all contrary opinion – and *prevent* free thought. *"No more debate"* is the defining statement of religio-political Controlling ideology

An *entirely unforeseeable* force of energy has now erupted into the world – without warning - and the *political climate* has changed; for "better or worse", a change that will be felt for decades to come. For the better, Climate Science can now be subjected to measured, *dialectical* scrutiny and the disingenuous AlGorythm brought to account. Beyond that there is no telling.

Human excess is always subject to revision, but predicting specific *effects* from questionable *causes* – *that cannot be questioned* - is dogmatic speculative fiction. To compromise the lives of millions in order to promote speculation, is cultural elitism - dressed as always in good intention. The road to Hell is paved with good intention; it doesn't get hotter than that.

"A" IS FOR GIRL

"Aphrodite - having craftily taken all her clothes off - was
declared the winner..."

Venus is the second closest planet to the sun, and next to it, the second brightest 'star' in the sky. It was named after the Roman goddess of beauty. To the Babylonians it was Ishtar "bright queen of the sky" and its Mesopotamian name Astarte was transformed by the Greeks into Aphrodite – goddess of love, beauty, pleasure and procreation. Its planetary symbol is assigned to all female life forms on Earth. It is the only female planet in our solar system and the only one still referred to as a star.

The Romans also appended the letter "A" to words denoting objects and ideas they considered female in nature, a tradition that continues throughout the Romance languages of Europe to the present day. The qualifier "La" usually precedes such words. Conversely, "A" is the letter most commonly attached to the *end* of female names: Anna, Barbara, Christina, Diana, Eva, Fiona, etc.

As the brightest object in the night sky, it is understandable that Venus would be described as a star. It is referred to as both the Morning star and the Evening star and in some cultures these were considered separate entities. It is the first to appear as the sun sets, and the last to leave when it rises. As ancient traditions would have it, it wakens the sun and puts it to rest. It is the image of a mother - a mother and sun. As with all mothers or potential mothers it necessarily embodies the female characteristics of beauty, love and procreation.

The fact that iterations of its name would include *Ishtar* and *Astarte* suggests why the planet and the *word* star are also connected. Astarte's symbol was in fact precisely a five-pointed "star" within a circle. How it was arrived at was a marvel of ancient astronomical insight.

The celestial qualities of Venus were known to many cultures, its motion, with respect to the sun and the Earth, was recorded by the Babylonians, Persians, Greeks, Romans and Maya. Because Venus is closer to the sun, its rotation around it is much quicker than that of the Earth: its orbital 'year' is 224.7 days compared to our 365 days. As a result, when an alignment occurs between Venus the Earth and the sun, it takes 584 days for the different rotations to catch up with one another and repeat it. If the alignment occurs in relationship to a specific zodiacal sign, it will take 5 such alignments over the course of 8 years before the same zodiacal sign is in the same relationship again. A geometrical representation of this cycle, connecting the points of alignment, is a pentagram - a five-pointed "star".

The symbol of the pentagram and its association with the female principle was known throughout the ancient world. As such its use as an abbreviation for woman or girl seems feasible. Though it was conceivably used before them, the Romans with their complex legal system, tax system, census taking and above all slave trading may well have used such a shorthand device to indicate "female". A star however is a complicated image to draw. An abbreviated version, in which the five points and the essential quality of the symbol are retained, makes more sense. This can be done with three lines to convey the same idea.

The Romans not only incorporated this symbol into their words to denote feminine quality, but also like many cultures chose it as the first letter of their alphabet.

"A" when pronounced "Aaaah" is the sound of breathing, both inhaling and exhaling. Women, as the means by which life is born into the world above all represent first breath – and by extension consciousness. It is only fitting that their symbol would be the first letter in the system of language.

In English, as every child knows, "A" is for Apple and as most of them also know it was an apple that got things started. Eve – as in Evening star – handed the apple of knowledge to Adam and self-awareness began. Eris the Greek goddess of chaos also set things off by throwing the golden "Apple of Discord" in front of the three goddesses Hera, Athena and Aphrodite. The apple read: *"For the fairest"*. Since the three ladies all considered themselves worthy of the title, the mortal Paris was elected to decide for them. Aphrodite

- having craftily taken all her clothes off - was declared the winner and in return Paris was given Helen of Troy. According to the Greeks, thus began man's first great war.

Venus, in her various manifestations, as beauty, love, pleasure and origin of life was also considered the origin of suffering and death. You can't have one without the other.

> *"... the kind of girl you want so much it makes you sorry*
> *Still you don't regret a single day*
> *Aaaah girl*
> *Girl"*

A SHRIMP

"As the camera tumbles on into the reaches of infinity..."

A while ago, scientists discovered sulfur-breathing shrimps existing in total darkness two miles down in the Atlantic. Their long held conviction that oxygen and light are prerequisites to life was proved to be wrong. More recently photographs revealed the possibility of water on one of the moons of Saturn, an inconceivable idea in the centuries that preceded it.

Do these discoveries make us more significant by virtue of our having made them, or less significant by revealing the scale of our ignorance and false assumptions? More significantly what is the cost of such so-called knowledge? How much physical suffering and anguish were required for us to establish yet more transitory conclusions? How much more is there to come?

As the camera tumbles on into the reaches of infinity, a shrimp in the darkness decides whether to turn left or right.

NONE SHALL PASS

"Penises, however, are often awake before their owners and long before the banks open..."

A few chastity belts are on exhibit in a few European museums, but they are few enough to suggest that their use was not widespread. There is also some doubt as to what that use may have been. There were no contemporary literary references at the time to what is surely one of the most remarkable items of female couture in the history of the world, and there were no precedents. The Romans and Greeks didn't mention them neither did the Persians, Egyptians, Chinese or Assyrians. They are generally associated with the Crusades of the eleventh, twelfth and thirteenth centuries, being worn apparently by European women as a deterrent to promiscuity, while their husbands were off fighting the Infidels.

The Infidels coincidently had the same problem, but they didn't go to such lengths to deal with it. They simply removed the anatomical parts that gave a woman pleasure then covered her up entirely - from head to foot. Any woman caught sneaking out was then stoned to death, an efficient solution, requiring minimal outlay and no maintenance.

Both Christianity and Islam marginalized the role of women, and the essential concern for both was the safeguard of property. Not the wife per se, but her means for producing heirs to promote and increase her husband's estate. The same means conversely that could be used to compromise said wealth by producing offspring other than his own.

Even though the crusader faced the same dilemma as his opponent, his ethical constraints prevented him from resorting to similar methods for solving it. That kind of thing was what made an Infidel an Infidel after all. To add to the difficulties, unlike his Muslim counterpart, a crusader was only permitted one wife to expend. His ingenious solution we are to believe therefore was to place his assets under lock and key. That being the case, the first question that comes to mind is where did he get such a device? Not from a shop, surely?

European nobility are not known for their ingenuity, but even if one of them had been inspired with the idea of a chastity belt, he would have needed someone else to make it for him - a metal worker of some sort, an armorer perhaps, or a jeweler. Since women occur in a variety of shapes and sizes, fitting the contraption would have been an essential part of the process - and necessarily a sensitive one.

Allowing a red-faced, stubby-fingered smithy to fuss around the wife's privy parts, making a tuck here and a tuck there seems highly improbable. On the other hand, it is unlikely that the Lord would simply spring it on his Lady wife as a fait accompli. Surprising a woman with a pair of shoes is an insane idea let alone a pair of iron drawers that aren't supposed to be taken off for years. The dutiful wife therefore would have to be on board with the idea from the outset. An idea proposed to her over breakfast maybe…

"Looks like rain, what?"

"Quite."

"Think I might round up a few of the chaps and bugger off for a while.

"Really?"

"Pop over to the Holy land. Give those damn wogs a thrashing."

"A splendid idea."

"Quite."

"Toast?"

"Certainly. So that's settled then. I'll have George stop by this afternoon and attach a metal contraption to your privates."

And the wife just said, *"Jolly good"* and that was that.

As a devout Christian presumably, she acknowledged the need for such measures, given her essentially wanton and deceitful nature as a woman as defined in the Bible. On the other hand, if she didn't agree, she could end up being strapped into a badly fitting, off-the-peg version whether she liked it or not.

Either way the plan went ahead. In the interest of propriety and to avoid the indelicacies of being fingered by the help, it's possible she tried on the device in private then suggested modifications and adjustments - the way wealthy Chinese women used to send a doll back and forth to the doctor with a note pointing out which parts didn't feel good. Or maybe the husband conveyed the information himself:

"Says it's a bit tight up around her bum here..."

Relationships between men and women vary in their expression, particularly with a couple that perceives wife as property this way. It would be most noticeable at the inauguration, the moment when the key was finally turned in the lock. One would think it might have been a romantic occasion, a fond wave goodbye so to speak, or simply one last use of the anatomical part in question to relieve the anxieties of the upcoming journey.

But if that were the case, it raises a very real concern: what if the wife were to get pregnant as a result, or if she was unknowingly pregnant already? Crusades weren't a five-minute affair. Things could get messy. A chastity belt blocks traffic in both directions. It would put things on a far more pragmatic footing. *Both* parties would *absolutely* want to make sure there wasn't a bun in the oven before they parted ways. Meaning there could be no sex for at least a month – for the wife that is. The good lord could always relieve his anxieties elsewhere – which in all likelihood, being to the manner born - he was doing anyway. Final lock down would have then been a perfunctory matter on a par with making sure the gas was turned off before going on holiday.

Suffice to say, on the day of departure, the little woman would be comfortably secure in her wrought iron jock strap, and her owner and liege - equally comfortable and secure – would be able to put his mind to the matter in hand. Together they would go forward to the greater glory of God, each of them armored in their way against the assaults of the unworthy: one to fight the Infidel, the other to fight infidelity.

The arrangement was strictly a one-way street, and the Holy Land is a long way from Putney. Unlike the lady wife, his lordship was not hampered by any such restraint as he set off through other people's back yards to do God's work.

The first crusade in 1095 was a resounding success. Jerusalem was captured and sacked, and all the Infidels along with their wives and children were tortured, raped and murdered - as were most of the Jews and Christians and *their* wives and children. A very loose interpretation of Christ's "*Suffer the little children to come unto me*" one would think.

In the fourth crusade, having set off in the usual way, the righteous arrived in 1203 at the gates of Constantinople - a Christian city - Orthodox Christian that is, not Catholic, a distinction based on their respective definitions of the number 3.

Constantinople hadn't been too happy about crusades two and three and wasn't about to change its tune this time around. In response, the devout Latins laid siege to the place, and when they finally broke in a year later, subjected it to the most appalling sack and pillage in recorded history.

The city at that time had become a *"veritable museum of ancient Byzantine art"* most of which the crusaders systematically looted or destroyed. The great library, with its countless ancient Greek and Roman artifacts, was also demolished, the *"greatest Church in Christendom"* looted and desecrated. By the time they were done, the prevailing Trinitarians had reduced the city to ruins and in the process raped and/or murdered most of the inhabitants.

It is the rank and file of course that perpetrates this kind of behavior. Rape is the product of frustration, and frustration increases the closer we get to the bottom of the social ladder. Class is about money, and frustration decreases commensurate with how much of it you have.

Penises however, are often awake before their owners and long before the banks open. They know no such distinction. Men are men regardless, especially when they are a long way from home.

The privilege of *Prima Nocte* was fashionable with the upper class around this time and must surely have extended to foreigners. If fucking the wives of his workers was the lord's God given right, then fucking the wives of men he wasn't dependent on at all was obviously a matter of course.

While the wife was back home struggling with the sanitary rigors of rusty underwear in an effort to repel all boarders, it is more than likely her husband was boarding other men's wives to his heart's content.

But the crusades weren't all fun and games, sometimes the godly got killed as well and that's where the real problem with chastity belts lies. His lordship presumably had the key to the device with him – or one of them – and he also had his armorer, which had its up side and its down side. While the armorer was there, he couldn't be coerced by the wife into making another set of keys. But since he *was* there, there was a chance he'd get killed. And if the Lord got killed with him, or simply *lost* his key, the wife was *really* screwed.

It is possible the husband had a contingency plan for just such an outcome. He may have hidden a second key somewhere around the manor and left sealed instructions to be opened in the event of his death. On the other hand he might as easily reason that if he was dead, what did his wife need a key for anyway?

The chances of this happening were at least 50/50. 50,000 men set out for the first crusade but only 20,000 came home. 10,000 died in battle, the rest were killed by Bubonic Plague

All in all, chastity belts make no sense in terms of what they were supposedly intended for. It is far more likely they were used as an *aid* to sex rather than a deterrent. The upper class may not be renowned for being smart, but they're notoriously kinky.

Boredom used to be something only the rich had to contend with, and elaborate sex games and the paraphernalia that went with them have been recorded from Nero to De Sade. A chastity belt fits right in with that tradition. As an elaborate foreplay device it would certainly kill time. Literally locking the door to the funhouse then hiding the key could stretch a two-minute fuck into an all day event. Or it could have been a party game. A half dozen, randy, Middle Age, drunks searching for the key to the prize: A girl named Chastity maybe.

Nowadays more and more people have time to kill and in keeping with that idea, 'chastity' belts are once again available in sex shops world wide - both for men *and* women. They can be built to order, in all likelihood, even out of wrought iron.

In the words of one Japanese salesman:

"Chastity belt is greatest invention for humankind"

SAMSON

"A guided muscle as it were - with a hair trigger..."

Examples of individuals renowned for physical strength are not common in the Bible. One whom most children are soon made aware of, however, is Samson, the revered Hebrew man of steel who would in time become the basis for the super heroes of today. Like them, his intellectual gifts were very much secondary to his physical prowess, in Samson's case, an imbalance that led to episodes of nonsensical violence comparable to the Terminator being played by Groucho Marx. Whereas most children know about his 'noble' end, few are familiar with his lunatic beginnings. What follows is the *entire* story, which occupies four chapters in the book called Judges.

Samson was born when the Israelites were once again behaving badly in the sight of the Lord. In keeping with all miraculous births, an angel alerted the parents beforehand. He also recommended a prenatal diet for mom and gave specific instructions regarding haircuts for the child. i.e., there should be none. Samson was then duly born into the world and as with all biblical big wigs, disappeared without trace until manhood. The first time we encounter him is when he is already interested in girls.

One day while wandering through downtown Tim-nath, Samson took a fancy to a particular Philistine gal, much to the concern of mom and dad.   A daughter in law who was uncircumcised so to speak, was not what they really had in mind for their only son. Despite their hand wringing however, Sammy insisted -

"Get her for me," he demanded, *"for she pleaseth me well."*

Unbeknownst to his parents, their son was on a mission from God. A guided muscle as it were - with a hair trigger; a means for old Yahweh to apply some of his stock in trade mayhem to the Philistines who were lording it up over His people. Having Samson marry one of them was His devious first move.

According to plan, the family set off to check out the potential daughter in law. Along the way a lion appeared, which Samson - as was his wont - dispatched without ceremony, tearing it asunder like a phone book. A particularly violent, and one would think *noisy* event that somehow went unnoticed by mom and dad. Blissfully unaware, they arrived in Tim-nath, had a quick chat with the girl, were sufficiently impressed and went home.

The next time Sammy went visiting, he was on his own, and on the way, discovered that the lion carcass was now full of bees! He ate a few handfuls of honey and on the return trip picked some up for mom and dad. For reasons to be revealed later, he didn't tell them where he'd got it. Their miraculous son conceivably did this kind of thing all the time, so they in turn didn't ask.

Dad then "went down unto the woman" and afterwards arranged a feast with the Philistines. Samson was assigned thirty men for the occasion and during the feast he decided to ask them a riddle. If they could answer it in seven days, he said, he would owe them thirty sheets and thirty changes of clothes. If not, they would owe him the same. The riddle was:

Judges14:v14. And he said unto them, Out of the eater came forth meat, and out of the strong came forth sweetness.

None of the thirty of course had any idea what the heck he was talking about and after a few days started to get nasty. They dropped in on the wife (who still didn't have a name yet,) and said if you don't tell us the answer, we're going to set you and your father *and* the house on fire! (Sheets apparently were hard to come by) The wife immediately set to weeping because *she* didn't know what the heck Samson was talking about either. He hadn't told mom and dad, why would he tell her? She was between a rock and a hard on, but the way women will, she stuck with him night and day until she got the answer. Right before the deadline - because "she lay sore upon him" - she succeeded. Incorrigible Philistine that she was, she then told the others.

When they gave Samson the answer, viz.- *"What is sweeter than honey? What is stronger than a lion?"* he became very "kindled." He realized right away what had happened. *"If ye had not plowed with my heifer,"* he said unto them, *"ye had not found out my riddle."*

(I'm a bit hazy as to the definition of a riddle, but having someone try to guess details of an incredibly implausible personal experience, known to no one except yourself hardly seems to qualify.)

Nevertheless, still kindled, Samson stormed off to a neighboring town, *killed* thirty of the inhabitants and took their clothes to pay the guests off. He must have screwed them on the sheets since they aren't mentioned. Having settled the account he then came home to find his wife in bed with his best friend!

Judges 14:v20 But Samson's wife was given to his companion, whom he had used as his friend."

A somewhat precipitous infidelity under the circumstances, which served to throw more sticks on the fire.

It was in fact her father's fault. Thinking that Samson was unhappy with his daughter for ruining his riddle, he'd passed her on to his best friend, then, hoping to make amends, offered his other daughter instead. (Philistine heifers it seems were interchangeable.) The offer further incensed our hero into tying two foxes together by their tails, setting fire to them and chasing them into the Philistines' corn. The ensuing conflagration spread to the vineyards and olives, leaving the Philistines no other option but to set fire to the ex wife and her father! To which Samson further responded by slaying the lot of them.

God's plan was coming along nicely.

Seeing the writing on the wall, *three thousand* men of Judah came to Samson and demanded he explain himself:

Judges 15v11. Then three thousand men of Judah went to the top of the rock of E-tam and said unto Samson, knowest thou not that the Philistines are rulers over us? What is this that thou hast done unto us? And he said unto them. As they did unto me so I did unto them.

"They messed with my riddle." in other words. The three thousand then promptly tied him up and marched him off to hand over to the Philistines.

God wasn't having any of this of course and cheating as usual, melted the cords "like burning flax.", whereupon Samson set about finding the "jawbone of an ass" and matter-of-factly dispatched a thousand men. Whether these were men of Judah or Philistines isn't specified, but it was thirsty work either way. As a bonus for carrying out His absurdly convoluted strategy of violent non-sequitors, God rewarded His boy by turning the self-same jawbone into a faucet!

Judges 15:v19 But God clave a hollow place that *was* in the jaw and there came water thereout.

Things calmed down for a while after that, until Samson happened to be strolling around Gaza one time, and another piece of ass caught his fancy; a harlot this time whom he readily went in unto.

Around midnight, after he was done, in keeping with his soccer hooligan M.O. he tore off the city gates, together with the pillars on either side, put them on his back and carried them to the top of a nearby hill. At that point, the locals decided it was time to have done with him once and for all.

As their luck would have it, Sammy found another piece not long after, up in the valley of Sorek, and when he'd done going in unto her that night, the city elders moved in behind him - each of them offering her eleven hundred pieces of silver if she discovered the secret of his strength.

This was plowing with heifer big time.

Delilah was her name, as every school kid knows, the sexiest babe in the Bible, the one who *betrayed* her man. Few of these children are aware of the psychotic violence and sexual shenanigans that had preceded the event, but all of them agree, she was a very *bad* woman.

Samson and Delilah were lovers. They were going at it like bunnies it seems, but they weren't married. As lovers do, after each go round they chatted and each time Delilah asked the same question: *"How come you so strong Sammy?"* In order to test her fidelity, Sammy in turn replied each time with a wrong answer. Three nights in a row the Philistines burst in thinking their man was disabled and each time Samson rousted them out of the tent. One would think infidelity had been fairly well established at that point, but on the fourth night, when Delilah complained that if he *really* loved her he'd stop lying to her about the way he could get his ass kicked, Samson finally fessed up:

Judges 16:v 17: ...if I be shaven, then my strength will go from me, and I shall become weak, and I shall be like any *other* man.

Everyone knows the rest: The Philistines grabbed him, blinded him, had a big feast to celebrate and put him on show for a laugh. In the final act of dumb versus dumber they chained him between two pillars - long enough apparently for his hair to grow back – and World Trade Tower style, he brought the house down. A finale that according to the Judges, resulted in more fatalities than he had caused in all his lunatic life.

And that was that: random violence and indiscriminate sex, end up under a pile of rubble having demonstrated no intellectual or spiritually redeeming quality whatsoever.

Such is the stuff of legend.

SOAP IN THE BUSH

"…as the music swells like an enormous bosom…"

When Baroness, Karen Von Blixen, aka "everywoman" Meryl Streep, discovers that the one brother she's in love with is not content with just doing *her,* and the other brother is busy doing everyone left over - including the servants - she decides that a change is in order. During a fashionable, upper class, Danish hunting spree in the snow, she propositions the second brother with a marriage arrangement: he gets funding for whatever he wants, in return for which, she gets what she wants: love - all that any woman wants. Brother Bror agrees.

For the occasion the Baroness has worn an enormous fur rimmed hat, which with its oval configuration and tipped up ends, can only be described as a giant, jauntily placed vulva. It is the first of the many hats and outfits to come, the cornerstone as it were, that encapsulates the entire thrust of the film. Its sexual connotation is obvious, but its darkness hints at the tragedies that lie ahead.

Its size confirms the underlying 'everywoman' conviction that they have the ultimate trump card – i.e. a vagina - and the manner in which it is displayed, reveals to us the elegance and style, which they, the gentler sex, bring to the world. Punctuating the idea, the Baroness concludes the discussion by shooting an unwitting life form flying overhead: a bird, possibly also female, possibly also with the same inherent conviction.

The change in order is Africa. Toot toot! Segue to a lusty steam train, forging through the arched expanse of a world in the throes of violation.

The train is stopped momentarily for Robert Redford, struggling with elephant tusks and the rigors of a wardrobe other than sport jacket and blue jeans. Interrupted from her own rigors the Baroness is introduced to the man of her destiny, a man who understands Limoges dinnerware - in Swahili no less: the mysterious American, blond heartthrob Dennys Finch Hatton. But the movie is just beginning. Dennys will not be climbing aboard at this juncture. He strides off into the expanse of endless nothingness in search of more things to mutilate. The Baroness watches him wistfully while tapping her internal barometer. There is moisture in the offing.

Nairobi: Metropolitan heart of the Dark Continent. White folks in suits and ties, black folks in their underwear. White folks in motor cars, black folks in the way. The Baroness discovers her own place in this world via the gentlemen's club where she is sternly informed that dress code above all requires the wearing of a johnson. A notion that obviously offends her everywoman conviction along with those of every woman in the theater and ignites a determination to have done with it before the end of the movie.

Bror arrives late from a philandering session to inform her that everything is ready and the wedding will take place in an hour. The horror! The gasps of the women in the audience are palpable. Weddings take *years* to plan! Poor Meryl! Who can save her?

Wardrobe of course - the other star of the film. An Oscar was presented on account of it, and one carriage of the train was devoted to carrying it. Cool as an African cucumber the Baroness appears in an off the cuff princess Di ensemble and our beating hearts are stilled.

In a part of the world that is, where most folks wear the same piece of string and a hanky all year round.

The wedding reception introduces us to the cast of upper class layabouts that run the show - raping, pillaging, and generally abusing an entire continent and its inhabitants. A gang of bored, backbiting, privileged spongers who welcome the occasion as an opportunity to get dressed up, drunk, lewd and overbearing. The fact these appalling human beings are there at all, is not questioned by the film for a moment.

In the midst of the mob, with the ring not yet warm on her finger, the Baroness intercepts her husband, mere inches from his first piece of extra mural 'conviction' and insists she be driven home. *"Yes dear"* says Bror, *"You'll love it here. The servants are wonderful"*

Domesticity is bad for movies. The wife is generally killed off at the beginning to avoid this bog of inertia in order to make way for the excitement of seducing her replacement. In Africa it's a little more colorful, but it's still to be avoided.

The Baroness has most likely never boiled an egg, so she has the enormous task of ensuring that her Kikuyu chef prepares cordon bleu to perfection. Her constant round of candlelight soirees demands no less. The chef is one of the many silly superstitious, childlike black folks, who must be instructed as to her every need. To add to her problems, the man of the house is rarely around, and during a brief visit – probably to change his underwear – announces that they won't be raising cows after all, but coffee. Before she can respond, he's out the door in search of fresh 'convictions'.

A superhuman womanly adjustment is now required and true to form Ms. Streep provides it. The female audience squirms with approval. Men are pigs! Apart from pissing over a six foot wall there's nothing they can do that women can't. Now he's gone, our plucky heroine can have what she deserves:

A *different* pig.

The domestic deadbolt slides back and she's out of the house! She plants acres of coffee beans, builds a schoolhouse, hires a teacher, teaches the children to sing God save the King, tries on a half dozen outfits, goes to a show and so on.

Feeling restless one afternoon she decides to do what all fine upper class layabouts do when they get bored: go shoot something. Coincidentally she bumps into Finch Hatton, who does such a thing on a daily basis, bored or not.

Before we know it, they're up in a plane together and on safari in a truck with the entire LL Bean catalogue in the back. After a day of shooting whatever takes their fancy, they retire to a meal served outside their sumptuous tents on a candlelit, linen covered table. And then - after a couple of bottles of Chateau whatever - the Baroness retires winsomely to her tent to prepare for the moment the audience has been waiting for: Bob is going to slip it to Meryl.

But the convictions have come home to roost.

Meryl has syphilis!

No matter says Bob sliding below camera...

The layered labial gauze of the mosquito net is all we see, as the music swells like an enormous bosom.

Then there's a war and a flood and the beans all catch fire. Bror needs money to marry someone else. Dennys's friend dies. The baroness goes back to Denmark. Then she comes back and Dennys dies. Finally she goes back to Denmark for good.

She receives news that two lions, one male, one female were seen sitting on Dennys's grave. It's a poignant, poetic image to take with us as we stumble into the street with our hankies. A man who made a career out of shooting lions and anything else that would turn a fast buck has been forgiven.

In the end we are all forgiven.

But do we get our money back?

HANDS

"…such a common occurrence that the good Lord has written in a charitable DNA clause.."

Wednesday morning, I pulled the garbage bins out into the street for collection. When I went back for the second one, I discovered a lizard had been sleeping under the first. In dragging out the bin, I'd chopped off its tail.

The lizard wasn't moving, it was cold, and being woken up like that must have been a bit of a shock. The tail on the other hand - a couple of inches in front of its face - was thrashing like a beached fish.

I wondered what it must feel like - waking up to find your tail in front of you like that - and not being able to look away? I bent over staring at it for a while, until I realized the neighbors might think I was acting strangely. I pulled out the other bins then went back for a final look. The tail was still as energetic. The lizard was still watching it.

It will grow back I thought, lizards are designed that way. Getting their tails chopped off is such a common occurrence that the good Lord has written in a charitable DNA clause. But *how* common I thought? More often say, than human beings having their *hands* chopped off - by other human beings? I doubt it. So why doesn't the good Lord - who devised this appalling human propensity - not recompense the victims with the same kind of charity? It hurt having them chopped off and a lot of them were children. Isn't that good enough?

What makes lizard tails so special? Lizards don't eat with their tails, don't defend themselves with them, or earn their livelihood, or dress themselves, or wash themselves or hold their children with them. They certainly don't to go to church and damn well *pray* with them. So what's the deal?

"It's cruel and unusual punishment (Joe) that's what it is."

"This is prison (Terry), it's supposed to be cruel and unusual. That's the whole idea."

(Billy Bob Thornton and Bruce Willis
in *Bandits*.)

TICONDEROGA

"Cheers."

The English army was 7,000 strong, including Germans, Indians, at least one pregnant woman and Baroness Riedesel and her three children. The American army was around 3,000 and they held the fort.

The English advance guard surprised the Americans whose commander ordered his men not to shoot. One of them was unable to restrain himself, however, causing everyone else to open fire. A single Englishman fell and the rest withdrew.

The Englishman was in fact unharmed and had simply fallen down drunk. The Americans took him back to the fort and placed him in confinement with one of their own who pretended to be a captured loyalist. The Englishman immediately revealed to him the English plan of attack and how many men there were.

The Americans spent the next day, July 4th, 'celebrating' the Declaration of Independence. The English meanwhile secretly hauled cannons up a hill overlooking the fort with which they could level it with ease. The Indians in the group, however, lit campfires that night and gave the game away. The Americans, realizing they were sitting ducks waited until the following night then sneaked off back to New York.

The American commander left a squad of men with cannons to guard pontoons in the lake and prevent the English from crossing. When the English finally arrived the Americans were too drunk to do anything.

The fort was taken without firing a shot.

Cheers.

THE WONDER OF ATLANTIS

"…a very shiny place apparently and noisy one would imagine during its construction…"

In their book *When the Sky Fell*, Rand and Rose Flem Ath present convincing evidence that Antarctica was in fact the mythical Atlantis. Taking their cue from Charles Hapgood's *Maps of the Ancient Sea Kings* and his theory of 'crustal shifts' they demonstrate that the island was once the temperate thriving hub of the world. A total shift in the earth's surface in 9,600 BC, resulted in its displacement to the current position at the pole where the culture was overwhelmed by water and ice.

This is the basis for the myths of the flood, and the idea of an original advanced civilization from the sea that crops up in the folklore and written histories of cultures around the world. According to the Flem Aths, the once flourishing and technologically supreme Atlantean/ Anatarctican civilisation was dispersed across the planet, replanting the seeds of essential culture in locations as varied as Peru, Mexico, Egypt and Cambodia. Here it erected huge, durable structures encapsulating the astronomical data that defined the sky to earth relationship at the time of the deluge. In an attempt, we are informed, to forewarn future generations should the same configuration reoccur.

Graham Hancock runs with the idea in his book *Fingerprints of the Gods,* then elaborates on it further in his illustrated travelogue *Heaven's Mirror,* on which he also collaborated with his wife, photographer Simaith Niin. Like the Flem Aths', the Hancock Niin documentation is equally plausible but they pivot their own theories on the even more remote date of 10,500 BC. A time they say, when the Egyptian Sphinx aligned exactly with the constellation of Leo at spring equinox and the ground plan of the three pyramids of Giza and the river Nile corresponded precisely to the Milky Way and the three stars in the belt of Orion.

Like the Mesoamerican civilizations and the far Eastern Cambodians the Egyptian building methods and immense knowledge of celestial mechanics are presented as evidence of a single originating culture. Both sets of authors catalogue their data in order to disprove the dates proposed by archaeological orthodoxy. A kind of cosmic finger wagging, aimed at humbling both expert and layman alike with evidence of comparable and often apparently superior technological know how to our own, that was already in existence as much as 12,000 years ago.

The four cultural groups have indeed left tantalizing possible evidence of this common cultural ancestor: massive megalithic structures, many of which defy modern attempts to explain their purpose or the processes by which they were accomplished. An achievement made possible say the authors, by the transfer of information from this protean culture that according to Plato erected large scale architectural marvels of its own.

Whenever Atlantis is evoked it is synonymous with splendor and intellectual accomplishment. It is a gleaming continent of sparkling white cities teeming with refined and magnificent inhabitants; a fabulous culture unparalleled before or since.

In his recollections of Atlantis, Plato described the main city as a circular configuration in which areas were accessed through a system of concentric canals. The opulence of these areas increased as the visitor approached the center. *"A wall of brass"* surrounded the outermost *"trader and mercantile"* rim followed by a *"wall of tin"* beyond which lay racetracks, parks and recreation areas. Next came a *"wall of Orichalcum"* a metal unique to Atlantis that *"sparkled like fire"*, and finally, a *"wall of gold"* behind which lay the central hub. It was a very shiny place apparently and noisy one would imagine during its construction.

On viewing all this splendor, a visitor's first question must surely be who actually did the work? And what were the terms of their employment? Quite apart from the enormous labor required to erect such marvels in the first place, maintenance must have been a monumental organizational undertaking. New York City's Parks and Recreation Department has an army of thousands dedicated to cleaning up trash, mowing the grass and watering the plants. A greater army of workers descends on the offices of that city every night to clean them. In the capital of Atlantis just polishing the walls must have been a full time job.

The folks who initiated and controlled all this, apparently resided in the rarefied Tiffinayesque gold inner circle. Who lived behind the sparkles of Orichalcum we are not told. The ones who bought and sold the materials – and presumably organized the workers as well - were the brass crowd on the outer rim.

The city was larger than Manhattan and the journey through it remarkably similar: a visitor's boat trip is comparable to a taxi ride up Broadway from Battery Park. He or she passes through the downtown financial district, continues up through the parks and entertainments of midtown, then finally arrives at the wealthy neighborhoods of the upper East and West sides.

Contemplating where the Atlantean workers lived, how they were paid and how they traveled to work inevitably points to the underlying social foundation to the glamour. Plato doesn't mention them in his account - not even the wall they lived behind. It seems that a city designed to such exacting aesthetics wouldn't allow a Bronx or a Bed/Stuy to mar the overall impression. Workers in all likelihood went about their personal lives far removed from the splendid city they made possible. Out of sight and out of mind as it were. Down wind and down *there* somewhere.

Meaning they would probably have to commute. There is no mention of buses, but the Atlanteans were big on boats. Possibly there was a ferry transit system. Then again, they were also big on circles and metallurgy. Maybe everyone rode shiny bicycles. More than likely they simply walked and they didn't get paid for the work at all. Given the great civilizations it supposedly inspired, the entire wonderful setup was probably predicated on slavery.

A jewel-encrusted city founded on a system of interlocking concentric canals is a phenomenal undertaking no matter how balmy it gets. How many workers did it take to damn up the polar ocean in order to build the retaining walls? Where did all the precious metal *come* from? Who *mined* it? Who *smelted* it? Who built and manned the *boats* necessary to import it? The continent of Antarctica is as big as the United States. Did the inhabitants grow their own food? And process it? If not who did? Were there other lesser civilizations around at the time? Proto-Peruvians, Egyptians, Aztecs? And how did the Atlanteans end up in charge anyway? Was there an ante-protean culture before *them* that passed the tricks along? And another one before that?

Who's on first?

Who is Number 1?

Such information if it exists at all is inconveniently buried under mile-thick polar ice, but the so-called legacy of its operating procedures is well known. The Aztec and Mayan oligarchies in ancient Central America maintained a brutal system of exploitation over a populace without recourse for thousands of years; every life outside the golden inner-circle subject to the discretion of unassailable whim. In one temple alone Cortes discovered the skulls of 130, 000 sacrificial victims. Children were especially useful for this business; assuaging the paranoia of self-appointed, self-serving superstitious posers.

Similarly the Egyptian Pharaohs and their priestly minions placed no restraint on the use of lesser human beings for their self-glorification. A five-thousand year, hereditary reich that committed all of its intellectual, technological and creative resources to clarifying the world beyond this one and the sky above it … at the expense of millions who benefited hardly at all from such indifference to earthly life, and to whom few if any monuments were dedicated. More space was devoted to birds and hippopotami on the walls of their temples than to acknowledging the countless anonymous souls who built them.

The Cambodians also configured their buildings to match celestial comings and goings. Like the Egyptians, Aztecs and Mayans they too spent a lot of time staring into space and joining the dots. They too decided that 'up there' is where you go to when you die, if you are rich that is, one of the in-crowd, one of the one's doing the finger printing. As both sets of authors would have it, this is the legacy of fabulous Atlantis. God king scams where the opulence of a few came at the expense of a never-ending supply of disposable human commodity.

The idea that such an insidious dynamic had its roots far farther back than we had previously imagined is hardly a cause for wonder, certainly not something to get hot and bothered about.

It is a terrifying, chilling thought in fact, inundating as it were. Like being overwhelmed by water and ice.

TROY

"Lawrence of Arabia - T.E. Lawrence - translated the *Odyssey..."*

King Priam is played by Peter O'Toole.

Peter O'Toole also played *Lawrence of Arabia*.

Lawrence of Arabia - T.E. Lawrence - translated the *Odyssey*.

He lived a few miles from Thomas Hardy.

Thomas Hardy wrote *Far from the Madding Crowd*.

The movie adaptation starred Julie Christie.

Julie Christie in *Troy*, plays Achilles' mom.

Achilles' son kills King Priam

King Priam is played by Peter O'Toole...

Directed by Wolfgang Petersen (*The Never Ending Story*)

NEW YORK GIANTS

"A cover up is no longer needed..."

In 1868, New York cigar-maker George Hull got into a discussion with an Iowa evangelist about the reference to giants in the book of Genesis. George was not a particularly religious man, but he was no slouch when it came to recognizing a God-given opportunity. As a result of the conversation, he determined to find the evidence that would prove the Bible 'right' and have some fun while he was at it. Wasting no time, he purchased a twelve-foot high, one-and-a-half ton block of Gypsum from Fort Dodge, Iowa and had it shipped to Chicago, Illinois. There, under his supervision, he had it carved into the likeness of a ten-foot tall, reclining, naked, human being - a likeness similar to his own as it happened - with a smile on his face to match. This 'petrified giant' was then surreptitiously transported by rail and by wagon to the upstate, New York farm of his relative William 'Stub' Newell, and buried behind his barn.

In the months that followed, several, 'million-year-old' fossils were suddenly discovered nearby. Whether George had anything to do with it isn't known, but the event certainly established a mood of credibility for such things in the neighborhood. When Stub decided it was time to dig a well on his property and unexpectedly unearthed what appeared to be the fossil of a giant human being, folks from nearby Cardiff were on the scene in a matter of hours.

By the end of that same afternoon, a tent had been erected and people were lining up to pay 25 cents a piece for a look. In the days that followed, crowds began arriving from as far way as Albany, Syracuse and New York City and George raised the price of admission to 50 cents. Experts appeared: Geologists, Paleontologists, Religious authorities and Native Americans, each paying their fifty cents and offering their opinions. It was a " fossilized giant", a "petrified Indian", an "aboriginal sculpture". It was remarkable. It was unique.

It was *huge*.

Apart from the Bible-thumping, religious fundamentalist fascination there was – for the ladies at least - the added perk of seeing male anatomy exposed on a grand scale. In promotional images released at the time, an obscuring branch or fig leaf fuelled the titillation. The equally-giant, clearly-defined member was unquestionably - both figuratively and literally - the centerpiece of the show, a show that became so popular that George was able to sell shares to a consortium of local businessmen for 37,500 dollars. The giant duo spelled money wherever they went, a godsend to shop keepers, hotel-owners, restaurant owners, bar owners and anyone else who could find a way to cash in on it.

When P.T. Barnum got wind of it, he offered 60,000 dollars to loan the giant for a year (that would be 1869 dollars.) Crafty George, however, figured he would make more on his own and turned him down. But George was dealing with the master now and not to be out-hoaxed, Barnum proceeded to have a copy made for his American Museum in New York City, presenting *it* as the 'original', and dismissing George's as a 'fake'. When the 'fake' finally arrived in the city, it was unable to compete with Barnum's 'original' and the consortium of businessmen, led by one David Hannum sued for damages.

In the course of the trial, the judge simply insisted George swear to the giant's authenticity and the jig was up. The case was thrown out and Barnum emerged unscathed. In response to the crowds that continued to line up to gawk at the fake-fake, David Hannum uttered the immortal *"There's a sucker born every minute"*, a remark that Barnum - to add insult to injury - also appropriated as his own.

The giant has had several homes over the years and is now at rest in the Farmer's Museum in Cooperstown, New York. Whether it is the original-fake or the fake-original is anyone's guess. Images from the time are conflicting and difficult to compare to the object now on exhibit. One thing is abundantly clear however: the remarkable centerpiece has apparently 'weathered' over time, the titillating details visible in the original pictures now reduced to an amorphous blob. A cover up is no longer needed.

Over time, all the details will fade, but to the perpetrators it is of no consequence. It achieved what it set out to achieve.

The smile will remain.

The bigger the lie, the more people believe it.

OVENSTUFFER PASSES

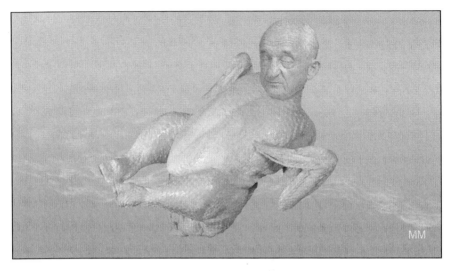

"…the efficiency of "manually strangling" the chickens…"

The death of the Frank Perdue revealed many insights into a feathers-to-riches career that according to *The New York Times* grossed 2.8 billion in its last year alone.

"It takes a tough man to raise a tender chicken," claimed the Frank and sure enough a local newspaper - which referred to him as a *"chicken magnet"* - talked about constant battles with his 19,000 employees.

On one occasion, lawsuits were filed by workers suffering from carpal tunnel syndrome. It cost the Frank a mere $40,000 to settle - a small price to pay for determining the efficiency of "manually strangling" the chickens.

Perdue employees quit their jobs 5 times more often than other Maryland workers on account of the injury rate being 10 times higher. On one occasion the Frank hired the New York mob to break up striking workers.

The secret to his golden brown birds was a diet of "*Marigold petals*" - and dye - available to them 22 hours a day since the lights were left on that long to encourage eating. Overhead fluorescents illuminated an individual living area about the size of a piece of Xerox paper. A single battery could house up to 30,000 inmates at a time, contributing to a yearly output of 2.6 million.

In answer to the old chestnut: "*How many chickens does it take to cross the road?*" in the Frank's case - from L.A. to New York – two every foot. With an average chicken standing 14 inches tall and 6 inches wide at the shoulder, in the thirty-five years or so since the Frank started to get up steam, this would amount to a solid wall of poultry from coast to coast, 7 feet high.

"WE HAVE TO TALK"

"... the fine, girlie, cop-asses jiggling ahead of me..."

"We have to talk": to a man, the four most terrifying words in the English language.

The Los Angeles Police Academy sits in the corner of Elysian Park, one the most beautiful parks in the city. Its palm-shaded hills and gullies and meandering roadways provide the perfect sandbox and exercise course for new recruits and fully-fledged officers alike. I drove through the park many times and once came up behind a squad of L.A.'s future finest jogging in formation. A half dozen, determined looking males were out front, followed deferentially at the rear by two females. I had to follow them for over a mile before they turned off, during which time the men pounded silently, doggedly ahead, and the women – who had no trouble keeping up – jabbered away to each other nonstop at the back.

Women accept that men do not talk as much, men accept that women talk a lot more- a whole lot more sometimes, often seemingly for no reason or the need to make sense.

It is a disparity that seems irreconcilable, suggesting something fundamental to the way we cope with the world. It occurred to me as I studied the fine, girlie, cop-asses jiggling ahead of me, that it has probably been that way for a very long time.

If we go with the Hunter/Gatherer paradigm, it is inevitable that men would take on the role of hunters and women the gathers. Size and upper body strength make males more efficient at running down and killing prey whereas the anatomical restraints imposed by breasts and wider pelvises make women less so. Childbirth and child rearing are also biologically determined female roles. (It seems unlikely there were many buff 'single' twenty year-olds out jogging with the guys in the Paleolithic.) As a result, human males and females would have often been physically separated from one another at times, as a matter of course.

As hunter, the human male became predator. His success in the hunt was contingent on stealth and strategy. Only essential information would be exchanged during the process and it would be directed with specific intent. Unnecessary sound would not only be contrary to the purpose but potentially life threatening. The survival of the tribe was dependent on successful hunting. It was subject to unpredictable, transient circumstances and competition from other predators. It was a timely and dangerous business. Talking – verbal communication – among males therefore, became inevitably imbued with characteristics of economy and efficiency.

For women, verbal communication was also essential to survival, but it would have been expressed very differently. Female humans encumbered with children and older family members were far more vulnerable than their male counterparts. Their inherently compromised mobility in fact made them potential prey to others - including out-group male humans. Unlike hunting, which requires stealth and strategy, gathering is a more methodical activity in which economy of sound is irrelevant to success. It nevertheless involves groups of individuals who must always be alert to danger and able to communicate it instantly.

Like it is for many other animal species, this is not always achieved through the use of sound per se, but by the sudden lack of it. By maintaining a constant level of chatter, the group is alerted to possible danger when elements within it go silent. It becomes an alarm signal for all to go silent and be on the look out.

For human females, the presence of sound - expressed through talking – would have represented a similar sense of wellbeing. What was said was almost irrelevant. Singing, laughing and seemingly undirected chatter all contributed to a feeling that things were okay - as opposed to the lack of it which probably meant they were not. Unquestionably many human females have fallen prey to other life forms – particularly human males. Over time therefore, silence and apprehension for women became synonymous.

Thousands of years later, hunting and gathering conditions have changed, but the essential natures of men and women have not. The deeply embedded verbal survival strategies particular to each remain.

Human females still strive to allay anxiety by constantly talking to one another - telephoning and texting, often just to verify each other's whereabouts. A teenage girl will rush headlong through barbed wire to answer a ringing phone and the threat of not being talked to by other girls can be her worst nightmare. Being ostracized by the group means that any anxieties she may have are now compounded because she cannot express them; she is already silent. And when they do get together, they still demonstrate the remarkable ability – to men - of being able to all talk at once without being confused. It's only when they start talking to men that their wonderfully effective strategy runs into difficulty - especially in the context of intimate relationships.

When that happens, 'more talk' meets 'less talk' head on. Lack of talk to females suggests something may be amiss, whereas to males it may imply nothing of the sort. On the other hand, to them, talking amounts to distraction unless something specific is to be achieved by it. Ironically, as most married men will concur, the process does in fact produce the result they want: quiet. It's just a roundabout way of getting there. Arriving at that conclusion can be a frustrating, time consuming business in which a female partner may throw all manner of unrelated information into the mix simply to sustain a level of sound interaction that makes her feel at ease. This is especially true when talking becomes argument.

As comedian Chris Rock points out, "...*it's impossible for a man to win an argument with a woman, simply because men*" – in keeping with the hunter paradigm – "*are handicapped by the need to make sense. Women aren't going to let sense get in the way of a good argument.*"

Women just "have to talk". It makes them happy. They feel secure. It's been that way for a very long time. It makes all the sense in the world.

You can't argue with that.

M-M-MOSES

*"*As *slaves* that is - *little girl* slaves. *"Have yourselves a b-b-ball"*

In the Stage Musical *The Ten Commandments*, Val Kilmer stars as –
or as the poster would have it – actually "is" Moses. According to
The L.A. Weekly, the production was originally "launched" in France,
and "...was the most successful show ever produced there." This is
hardly surprising and should not have influenced the decision to buy
a ticket. In Hollywood, grandiose claims are par for the course. The
fast food joint up the street from where I lived had a marquee out
front that read: "In L.A. everyone eats at Rick's."

The real surprise in the article, is the reference to the play's director
Robert Iscove in which he characterized his production as "*...an
important story about mankind's quest for a more peaceful existence.*"

The quest for peace is unquestionably a noble enterprise, but
"mankind" suggests a universal idea. In light of Moses' career, it is a
claim that's difficult to reconcile with the facts, and even harder to

visualize in terms of finding something to sing about. I didn't see the musical, but I have read the book.

The very notion of transposing Biblical text, i.e. the purported actual word of God, into song and dance seems both questionable and problematic. Words spoken by God Himself may be open to interpretation, but surely, by no means can they be subject to change, much less for the sake of making them rhyme. "Taking my name in vain" was one of His touchier directives.

Biblical events cannot be altered, to do so undermines the fundamental premise of the Book. This is history as declared by God himself, not a John Grisham novel. If the show strays from the facts, then both it and its precedent are invalidated in terms of essential truth. In that regard, as a musical production, the story of Moses would have had to come to terms with one incontrovertible difficulty right up front. Alluded to in the Bible, and later confirmed by Midrashic scholars is the fact that...

Moses had a stutter.

Which is why Aaron did most of the talking. The reason for this impediment is not revealed in Biblical scripture, but *is* nevertheless – according to Avivah Gottlieb Zornberg in her hefty *Reflections on Exodus* – a matter of accepted fact *"according to a famous legend."* To whit:

The Egyptian high priest Balaam (later famous for his talking ass) tried to convince Pharaoh that the three-year old Moses spelled trouble, and that he should kill him. The angel Gabriel, disguised as one of the priests, interceded and suggested a test. He placed a burning coal and an onyx stone in front of him proposing that if he were a normal child, he would go for the "shiny" one – the coal. If he were tricky, he would go for the valuable one. Moses who is *"indeed precociously wise"* naturally reached for the stone, but at the last moment, Gabriel, "supernaturally" forced his hand toward the coal. Which Moses picked up, and, just like babies do (apparently) stuck in his mouth; saving his life but causing him to talk funny thereafter.

The sum result as far as the show is concerned, is that in order to remain true to the *facts*, Kilmer's musical rendition of Moses could only amount to a two hour version of The Who's *"M-m-my G-g-generation."*

As Cecil B. De Mille pointed out in his unprecedented on stage/on screen introduction to his movie of the same name: *"Nothing is known of the life of Moses, from the days of his infancy until his early thirties or thereabouts."* Even so, he was able to construct an entire film – or as he proposed it, "a *documentary*" – around this discrepancy, complete with dialogue. Based, he informed us, on the writings of Philo and Eusebius, who based their writings in turn, on books *"that have since been lost or destroyed."* An explanation, right up there with the d-d-dog ate the homework.

What the Bible tells us is that the infant Moses was spotted by Pharoah's daughter Bathia, as he floated down the river in a basket. (Just like Hindu Krishna, Babylonian king Sargon and Romulus and Remus) Her father, had just ordered the murder of all newborn

Hebrew boy children, and Bathia realizing that the child must have been placed in the river to escape such a fate, decided to save his life and adopt him as her own. An absurdly suspicious arrangement under the circumstances, that nevertheless went unheeded by the rest of the family – compounded by the fact that she also gave the child a Hebrew name. (The same implausible scenario would be reprised centuries later when king Herod, who had also just pulled the 'kill all the baby boys' routine, is informed by certain "Wise-men" that a star, no less, has led them to the one child who has escaped… which was at that moment *pointing* at the stable where he was at!)

When the Israelites were first *invited* to Egypt (to escape famine) there were 70 of them – a recurring number in Israelite history: 70 scholars translated the first five books of the Bible and the Torah has 70 faces etc. The original group comprised the father and relatives of Joseph – at that time a financial muck-a-muck and top adviser to the Pharaoh. Through his influence, which was clearly significant, they were given the lush territory of Goshen as their own in which to settle. Rather like a bunch of hungry folks showing up in America and being given the state of California.

Five generations later, there were around 2 million of them, in the course of which supernatural reproductive behavior, (A song opportunity if ever there was one) they had stopped being 'guests' and become 'slaves.' How and why this happened is not specified. They were clearly healthy slaves, however, with a lot of spare time on their hands, and based on their later laments in the desert, not so badly off:

NUMBERS 11:v.5. We remember the fish which we did eat in Egypt freely: the cucumbers, and the melons, and the leeks, and the onions, and the garlic.

NUMBERS 16:v.13. Is it a small thing that thou hast brought us up out of a land of milk and honey, to kill us in the wilderness...?

And when they were leaving:

EXODUS 12:v.38. And a mixed multitude went up also with them; and flocks and herds, even very much cattle.

This would be their *own* cattle. Yahweh in His exuberance had specifically killed all the Egyptian cattle *twice* during His unholy onslaught of afflictions. Once with the Murain, a kind of foot and mouth presumably, and then when they were *already dead*, again with a hail of brimstone. Redundancy aside, the fact that He was able to pinpoint only the Egyptian cattle is noteworthy. If He was that discriminating with cows, why was it necessary to go through the elaborate rigmarole of identifying the Egyptian firstborn during Passover?

The catalogue of plagues is too well known to itemize – although difficult to imagine singing along to. Suffice to say that once the firstborn Egyptian children are all murdered the Israelites are free to leave; an opportunity for an all-out looting spree during which the Egyptians – who are busy mourning over their children – are relieved of all their valuables.

Practical concerns like food or tents etc., are ignored in the text, but with "600,000" of their men fully armed, and carts loaded to the hilt with swag, the Israelites set off in search of the Promised land: a choice piece of property up the coast, that God has picked out Himself for them as compensation for the difficulties experienced in Egypt. Oddly enough the same land they had abandoned in the first place, which is now also "flowing with milk and honey." The snag of course was that it happened to be someone else's milk and honey, namely the people who were living there, a mere technicality, which God assured His folks would easily be overcome, once they arrived, At that time, He would help them slaughter everyone in sight, and the milk and honey and everything else would be theirs. The man to lead them and organize this surprise carnage was Moses, to whom God conveyed His instructions directly:

DEUTERONOMY 7:v.1. When the Lord thy God shall bring thee into the land whither thou goest to possess it, and hath cast out many nations before thee, the Hitites, and the Girgashites, and the Amorites, and the Canaanites, and the Perizzites, and the Hivites, and the Jebusites...

2. And...thou shalt smite them, and utterly destroy them; thou shalt show no mercy unto them...

Gaza is less than 300 miles from Goshen (closer than LA is to San Francisco) but with God in charge, Moses leading the way and a pillar of smoke and tower of flame up ahead to guide them, it takes the Israelites *forty years* to get there. Instead of going directly east, the whole kit and caboodle unaccountably went south – into the desert.

God moves in mysterious ways indeed, a song and dance number without question.

The Arabian Peninsula was densely populated at this time apparently, and in the course of the forty years of wandering, there were many encounters with local folk along the way. One of the first was with the Midianites, a nostalgic moment one would think for Moses who had fallen in love in Midian and married his Midianite wife there. His only son had also been *born* there – certainly a cue for a poignant melody one would think, but not so. Moses uses the occasion instead to thoroughly demonstrate his "quest for peace" methodology.

> NUMBERS 31:v.7. And they warred against the Midianites ... and they slew all the males.
>
> 9. And the children of Israel took all the women of Midian captives, and all their little ones, and took the spoil of their cattle, and all their flocks, and all their goods.
>
> 10. And they burnt all their cities wherein they dwelt, and all their goodly castles, with fire.
>
> 14. And Moses was wroth with the officers ...which came from the battle.
>
> 15. And Moses said unto them, Have ye saved all the women alive?
>
> 17. Now therefore kill every male among the little ones, and kill every woman that hath known man by lying with him.
>
> 18. But all women children, that have not known man, by lying with him, keep for yourselves.

As *slaves* that is. *Little girl* slaves. *"Have yourselves a b-b-ball"*

This was early on in the proceedings, only a couple of months after the "Thou shalt not kill" directive. There were still thirty-nine more years to go...

> DEUTERONOMY 2: v.34. And we took all his cities (Sihon) at that time, and utterly destroyed the men, and the women and the little ones, of every city, we left none to remain.
>
> 35. Only the cattle we took for a prey unto ourselves, and the spoils of the cities which we took.

> DEUTERONOMY 3:v. 3. So the Lord our God delivered into our hands Og also, the king of Bashan and all his people; and we smote him until none was left to him remaining
>
> 4. And we took all his cities at that time there was not a city which we took not from them...
>
> 6. And we utterly destroyed them, as we did unto Sihon...utterly destroying the men, women and children of every city.

(N-n-next time you're out shopping, look at the families around you and p-p-picture this idea. And maybe sing while you're at it.)

> JOSHUA 6:v. 21. And they utterly destroyed all that was in the city, (Jericho) both man and woman, young and old and ox, and sheep, and ass, with the edge of the sword.

24. And they burnt the city with fire, and all that was therein; only the silver and the gold and the vessels of brass and of iron, they put into the treasury of the house of the Lord.

JOSHUA 8:v.24. And it came to pass when Israel had made an end of slaying all the inhabitants of Aiin in the field, and in the wilderness where they chased them and when they were all fallen on the edge of the sword...
25. And so it was, that all that fell that day, both of men and women, were twelve thousand, even all the men of Aiin.

JOSHUA 10:v.20. And it came to pass, when Joshua and the children of Israel had made an end of slaying them (the Amorites) with a very great slaughter, till they were consumed...
26. And afterward Joshua smote them, and slew them and hanged them (kings of the Amorites) on five trees...
28. And that day Joshua took Makkedah and smote it with the edge of the sword. and the king thereof he utterly destroyed, them and all the souls that were therein; he let none remain.

And so on and so on: a relentless catalogue of premeditated carnage, fairly well summarized at the end of the chapter, but not confined to it:

JOSHUA 10: v.40. So Joshua smote all of the country of the hills, and of the south and of the vale, and of the springs, and all their kings; he left none remaining, but utterly destroyed all that breathed, as the Lord God of Israel commanded.

"Utterly" it seems, would be the show's defining number. Chapters 11 and 12 of Joshua read like a warehouse inventory, listing countless kings "utterly" smitten, cities "utterly" destroyed, and men, women and children "utterly" slaughtered – and of course, swag "utterly" taken.

A number one hit, undoubtedly.

In any other military context it could be argued that all this violence may have occurred in self-defense. But God's original directive to the Israelites ahead of time, about smiting everyone they run into and destroying them without mercy, clearly determines that the outcome of any and all encounters was a foregone conclusion. Contrary to director Iscove's grandiose claims, *"mankind's* quest for a more peaceful existence" just isn't in the script.

As with all popular accounts of Moses, the *forty-year* rampage in the desert is left out entirely: neither the Musical *Ten Commandments*, De Mille's *Ten Commandments*, Aviva Gottlieb Zornberg's *Reflections on Exodus*, Eli Wiesel's *The Story of Moses* nor the countless storybooks and animated cartoons mention it at all.

Only the *Bible* – the *"indisputable word of God"* Himself – does that.

An Inc-c-convenient Truth if ever there was one.

S.E.T.I.

"And what does an athlete do?" asked the Alien, *"What service does he perform?"*

"*And who amongst you,*" asked one of the Aliens, "*is the most revered, the most recognizable to your fellow Earthlings?*"

"*There is one,*" said the president, "*who is truly revered, an athlete whose face is recognized more than any other on the planet.*"

"*And what does an athlete do?*" asked the Alien, "*What service does he perform?*"

"*An athlete entertains us and inspires us with the idea of winning.*" answered the president. "*They are individuals that humans respect and look up to.*"

"*And who is this one you refer to? What precisely is the nature of his winning?*"

"*His name is Muhammad Ali, and he is a boxer.*"

"And what does a boxer do? How does he inspire?"

"A boxer is a human being who enters a small square enclosure with another human being in which they hit each other until one is beaten unconscious or so badly injured he can hit no more. That man is considered the loser and the other the winner. Muhammad Ali has been a winner many times and is very clever and amusing in his style. He is admired by us all."

The president turned to call the boxer forward to meet the Aliens. When he turned back, they were gone.

AN ANT

"...as remote and beyond my control as a leaf falling from a tree in China..."

I watched an ant, stumbling across the hairs on my arm, a scene as remote and beyond my control as a leaf falling from a tree in China. I had no say in any of it.

Even if I were to fool myself that this wasn't so by brushing the ant away, I'd still be left with the arm. The arm: with its impenetrable jungle of hairs, each one unique, purposeful, unaccountable, utterly, fundamentally incomprehensible.

I wondered if such a sense of helplessness might have occurred to the ant, right before everything disappeared.

PLAYING THE GAME

"… the only places the ordinary Joe could legitimately get a good
look at breasts and bottoms…"

The publicity photograph shows him standing barefoot in a business suit, hanging by one arm from the branch of a tree. His passion, we are told is Conservation. His career has spanned several decades, during which he has photographed the glamorous, the rich and famous, and most significantly, the wildlife and people of Africa. The combination of these subjects constitutes the material for the show.

According to photographer Peter Beard, elephants are analogous to humans in their social behavior, their family structure, even in the kinds of diseases they have become prone to - particularly heart disease. Due to increased deforestation they are becoming more and more confined to what he describes as "ghettos". As a result of this confinement, within increasingly smaller and smaller areas, they have also come to exhibit the same destructive tendencies as humans: they destroy the environment irreparably.

To demonstrate the extent of this destruction and give us some idea of its tragic consequences Beard creates photomontages- sometimes very large- presenting us with a kind of before and after narrative. Elephants are shown destroying trees, alongside photographs of elephant bones and dead elephant babies. Old photographs of 'white' game-hunters posing with their trophies are juxtaposed with images of wildlife and indigenous African peoples, including images of beautiful African women, who are often bare-breasted.

Photographs of naked women used to be hard to come by. National Geographic Magazine and scientific studies of native peoples, were once the only places the ordinary Joe could legitimately get a good look at breasts and bottoms. It was also one of the few ways for photographers to justify an artsy 'feel-up'. Early pictures in order to de-emphasize this idea often showed front and side views, to impress on the viewer the strictly anthropological nature of the study.

Making a large photograph of a naked black woman the focus of a montage about conservation seems to be a continuation of that convoluted strategy. In terms of a selling tool, it also functions in the same way as beautiful women posing alongside automobiles. Even though it supposedly contrasts the 'white' man's arrogant destructiveness with the 'black' woman's victimized purity, when it comes down to it, it's still a really big picture of a great-looking gal with nice tits.

Beard's friendship with Baroness Karen von Blixen leads to her being included as one of the photo subjects. This sells the art in a different way. The movie *Out of Africa* is part of the American experience: a tragic love story set against the backdrop of sweeping African landscapes, starring two of Hollywood's great screen idols. The image of the real-life heroine of that story can't help but evoke similar emotions.

When I went to Karen von Blixen's house in Kenya, which is now a museum, what was actually evoked was the image of white privilege. Not just over blacks but other whites as well. She embodied the upper class prerogatives of European society, the sense of superior claim that initiated the colonial process in the first place. Enormous land grab and theft of material resources understandably prompted some kind of ethical justification - these were God fearing folks after all. They convinced themselves they were acting from the most pious of motives: the white man was raising the simple African from some kind of moral and civilized torpor, a duplicity implied in the movie but completely obscured by sentimentality. The film opens with Blixen shooting wildlife and she meets her lover Finch Hatton as he loads his elephant tusks onto her train. Their romance is consummated on safari. Photographs of her promote the art with 'celebrity' while contradicting it with 'complicity'.

Beard augments his images with poignant hand written declarations. This is an emotionally charged device. It suggests spontaneity, sincerity, and in its struggling, uneven, formation, the human frailty and desperation of the artist's message, a message in a bottle as it were, a plea from the heart sent out to each of us personally. And to ensure that we truly understand the gravity of his message, he punctuates it with blood, huge swatches of it, thrown, daubed, smeared and dripped over everything. No one can dispute the authenticity of a conviction signed in blood. But is the idea of such a message not a continuation of the same white missionary zeal, the same sense of superior European insight that initiated the process?

Few art gallery goers will argue against conservation, but what kind of people can afford to pay $75,000 for a picture of it? - besides banks, corporations, galleries and the rich and famous, the very people who have a vested interest in the status quo: the wealthy people in the photographs.

The Africans in the images are fading as surely as the wildlife, victims of the same inexorable process of commodification. By Beard's own definition, these are the images of their "dying breath". Like insight, awareness, conservation - and extinction – it is just one more thing to be exchanged across a counter. It has a price.

It is a dilemma that has confronted countless photographers when faced with a situation of human tragedy: the impulse is to record it - and then sell it. Starving children, refugees, war victims, homeless people equal money to be made from suffering, the justification being, that it must be recorded for posterity. But whose posterity? There are pictures of bodies at Gettysburg, starving Indian families in the 1800's, the women and children of Mylai and on and on. Whose purpose do they ultimately serve?

Peter Beard's photographs of wildlife and the people of Africa are exquisite. When combined in this way, however, they become the image of something very different. They are a record of what has come to pass, but what exactly is to be conserved?

MOUTHS TO FEED

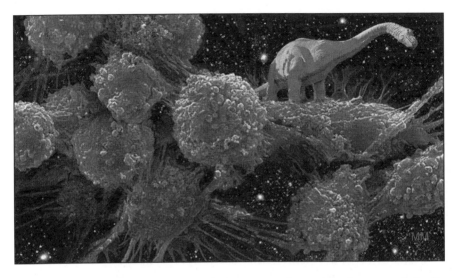

"...the possibility, that in the future everything may be revealed..."

Corporations are considered living organisms and afforded rights accordingly. Their primary directive, like all life, is to increase. Unlike biological organisms, however, their methods are not constrained by a fear of physical suffering or demise. To exist as a corporation is not a matter of life and death in a literal sense. They are as a result, a form of organism that is not directly accountable for its actions. Their compulsion to increase is an appetite without restraint.

As with any feeding arrangement, that which is consumed ends up being part of the consumer. *Incorporated* that is. The chicken that gets eaten today may be helping perform brain surgery or driving a bus tomorrow, etc. What is unique to the corporate organism is that the chicken it eats - or more precisely that which produces the chicken - *wants* to be eaten.

The so-called third world, that produces for very little and consumes relatively little, wants to be on the first world, eating end as well. Since the corporate organism is compelled to increase, it cannot help but oblige. This is surely a self-defeating dynamic. More and more producers will become consumers until eventually there will be no producers left. The organism will starve.

When large organisms and extinction are evoked, we invariably think of dinosaurs. Size was what did them in we are told, they just got too big for their own good. They too were corporations with enormous appetites. Recently that idea has been revised: a giant asteroid hit the earth instead we are now told and they all choked to death in the dark. A far more exciting, pyrotechnic, Hollywood-type ending in keeping with today's need for instant results.

Whichever it was, the fact is, dinosaurs *did* get very big. The question is, did they have anything in common with Walmart and Exxon? Did they consume without restraint? Is it even possible for a biologic organism to get too big for its own good? Since there are no dinosaurs left, maybe elephants are a good place to start. They're big. They eat a lot. Can they be getting *bigger*?

The African Elephant, weighs between 4 and 7 tons. In order to sustain that bulk it requires 300 to 500 pounds of food a day. In order to consume that much, it must eat non-stop for 16 to 20 hours. That's a restraint. There just aren't enough hours in the day to eat any *more*. As far as size goes, it is likely modern Elephants are maxed out.

The biggest mammals on the planet are whales. The Blue Whale, by far the biggest and heaviest, weighs in at around 120 to 170 tons and measures over 80 feet in length. This is comparable to several of the Sauropod dinosaurs such as Brachiosaurs and Apatosaurs. The Blue Whale consumes between 4000 and 6000 pounds of food a day. That is, between 2 and 3 tons, or 3 to 4% of its body weight. It does this basically by absorbing it like a giant vacuum cleaner. It doesn't chew the food but strains it through its baleen plates like a sieve. This gives the whale the edge over elephants and dinosaurs since chewing takes time – and energy. It also has the key advantage of not having to deal with gravity in the same way.

With water to support it, the whale doesn't need the complicated apparatus of legs. Legs require considerable additional fuel to operate, particularly in the case of Sauropods where they have to transport the same kind of tonnage. Elephants suffer from arthritis on that account as well as heart disease so it seems likely jumbo dinosaurs may have had the same problem. Whale sleep patterns are similar to humans and elephants so they too have restraints regarding how long they can spend eating. They probably aren't getting any bigger either. 160 million years from now things might be different, but given that humans are working hard to make sure a lot of whale species don't make it to the end of the century, the question is moot.

Which brings us to dinosaurs.

Brachiosaurs and Apatosaurs reached lengths of 80 feet and weighed between 50 and 80 tons. Based on the discovery of 8 and 9 foot long shoulder blades, paleontologists propose that there may have been far larger animals still: 130 feet long possibly. Creatures they refer to as Ultrasauruses, the relative weight of which would be way over 100 tons. These animals had essentially the same diets as modern elephants even though they were ten, twenty, maybe even thirty times bigger.

When we transpose elephant statistics to these kinds of dimensions, we encounter the same kinds of dietary requirements as the Blue Whale. What distinguishes the Blue Wale however is a mouth that is so large it can engulf material equal to its entire body mass. This is far from the case with Sauropods. It's not the *availability* of such staggering amounts of food that is a problem or even the time that it takes to consume it; it is simply the *ability* of the animal to incorporate it.

Based on the evidence, it doesn't seem possible.

If it takes an elephant an entire day to eat a mere 500 pounds, it should take a 50 ton dinosaur twelve and a half-times that long, which is absurd. Unless, that is, it had a head twelve and a half times as big as an elephant's, or in the case of 130 foot monsters- twenty-five times as big. But it didn't...

It was smaller.

Dinosaurs and cows have very little in common. The average weight of a Jersey cow is 960 pounds and it eats between 30 and 40 pounds of food a day, which is approximately 3 to 4% of its body weight. Its legs are narrow, its neck is short and it has a small skinny tail. An 80-foot Apatosaurus on the other hand, has enormous legs, a fifteen-foot neck and a twenty-foot tail. A Diplodocus is 88 feet long with a similar configuration. What's remarkable about them is that despite their size, they both have heads roughly as big as – or as small as - a cow's.

That's a restraint:

How can a cow's head get two and a half *tons* of leaves or whatever down its throat in a day?

Not surprisingly, dinosaur 'experts' are baffled by this question: *"It is likely that they ate constantly, pausing only to cool off, drink or to remove parasites."* they say. As the above demonstrates this is hardly an answer. Pausing for anything doesn't even seem an option. Conceivably dinosaurs were *incredibly* fuel-efficient. If they ate non-stop like elephants, with the same size intake-mechanism, the body size to fuel size ratio of an 80-ton dinosaur, would have been 130 to1. In automotive terms: 130 miles to the gallon as opposed to an elephant's 24.

Which brings us back to Walmart and Exxon.

Corporations also strive to make acquisition and distribution of resources more efficient and economical - with the least possible outlay for the greatest possible return. It is a dynamic we all strive for. How a brontosaurus supported itself is anybody's guess. What distinguishes a corporate organism is that it is not constrained by the *size* of its mouth.

Size is a human preoccupation based on individual significance not overall scale. Ants en masse, far out-size humans. It is a matter of scope, the scale of the *compulsion* to consume. It is the appetite of the *species*, a species in our case that is proliferating unchecked. For that there is most definitely a corporate precedent. Seen as a total organism, the human relationship to the environment is comparable to that of one of the 'smallest', most voracious forms of eater, one that demonstrates the same unrestrained determination to increase.

Cancer consumes as much as it can, for as long as it can until its host – the producer - can no longer provide. Then both die. Cancer, however, is not distracted, as far as we know, by the sense of its own mortality. Above all by the conviction there is purpose beyond the moment. There is no fear of jeopardizing the possibility that in the future everything may be *revealed*, that everything will be shown to have been worthwhile ... entirely for our benefit even. Cancer is concerned with now, with the idea of being. Unlike us, there are no individuals among its ranks worrying over the nature of the dynamic of which they are a part. It is a corporation consuming without restraint, but there are no cancer "Uh oh" moments on the brink of oblivion.

GUNG HO

"Whitey wouldn't take a *bath* for another 1200 years…"

When we came up with the idea of freewill, we pulled the rug out from under ourselves and started wearing it as a hat. It is our most cherished conceit. In a moment of inspired bravado we went over the wall from the rest of nature and we've been on the lam ever since. Our newfound freedom imbued us with a superiority regarding all other life and an even greater sense of unique ultimate purpose.

By assuming this position, however, we effectively separated ourselves from ourselves. Part of us it turned out, had stayed behind. Whereas some things seemed to be definitely under our control, others most assuredly were not. A dispute within each of us ensued in which we attempted to reconcile the dilemma. Thousands of years later, it is still going strong. Being creatures of two minds has complicated our sense of self no end; even the 'smartest' among us are at odds with themselves.

Carl Sagan once remarked that *"We are the first species to have taken our evolution into our own hands"* but when asked whether we should extend that sensibility into space he replied, *"...we have no choice...we are genetically compelled."* Similarly, Nietzsche contended that *"A thought comes when it will, not when I will."* but then went on to say that man's *"essence, his actions, his entire single, inevitable, and irredeemable reality – is a voluntary achievement, something willed..."*

This 'on the bus/off the bus?' predicament expresses itself most clearly in the ongoing debate between "Science" and "Religion", the latter being the greatest promoter of "freewill" and Science that of genetic determinism. Both sides, however, espouse aspects of the opposing point of view, resulting in a convoluted state of antagonism that appears impossible to resolve. We have become in effect, the only organism on the planet that is perpetually off balance. Quantum physics suggests that we can be in two places at once, but it has little to offer about being in *one* place at once with two opposing states of mind. It doesn't as yet even have a handle on "we", a shortcoming that becomes that much more evident when "we" consider what "we" will say to 'alien' life forms.

Carl Sagan was one of the foremost proponents of the search for extraterrestrial intelligence and instrumental in the launching of the Voyager spacecrafts to that end. I happened to illustrate *The New York Times'* article about the *"Earth's Greatest Hits L.P."* that he and his associates had assembled and placed onboard. Considering what actually went onto the record, the definition of 'intelligence' struck me as remarkably shaky.

The disc was encoded with images as well as the 'sounds' of Earth and it goes without saying that the most relevant would be those of the things that had made it: human beings that is, in their various historical and ethnic get-ups possibly, but most importantly in their simple, unadorned state. The idea of a naked man and woman, however, was not acceptable to the committee in charge, and they were shown instead only as black silhouettes. There were photographs of various ethnic groups and natural phenomena, but none of the actual process that occasions human life... much less the workings of the parts involved. The plaque on the outside of the craft did show line drawings of a naked man and a woman, but after much hand wringing and soul searching apparently, the tiny single line indicating the woman's vulva was removed. Any alien intelligence with half an ounce of insight would undoubtedly be amused by our apologetic sense of self. On the other hand, the idea that aliens even have such faculties as humor and insight is simply par for the hypothetical folly. Images of human beings shown to some ethnic groups on *this* planet make no sense to them – even images of themselves.

The mindset that contemplates space travel is a mixed bag encompassing the full range of convictions regarding humans' sense of self and their relationship to the rest of nature, but it is from out of it that a delegation will be organized to communicate with "intelligences" other than our own. The question is: what do we say in the unlikely event something or someone actually responds to the messages we've sent? How does such a confused and confusing consensus explain itself?

Science takes pride above all in constantly reevaluating its findings, a kind of honesty that it levels against religion, which does not. But scientific theory by its own definition is only ever a temporary expediency. It is always subject to revision as new discoveries are made. Under those terms, all knowledge is inherently false, simply because it is *always* incomplete. Explaining anything with umpteen other human voices in disagreement is difficult enough, but it is compounded by the possibility that the scientific know-how we think we possess may even become obsolete during the course of the transmission.

At this point in time, according to astrophysicists, it all started with a Big Bang, a phrase that not only seems grossly inadequate for an event of such significance, but also a contradiction in terms. "*In space no one can hear you scream*" we've been told, let alone hear a "bang" … no matter how big it is, or how close the listener's ear might be. Given that the first humans who would conjure up the notion of bangs were "13.7 *billion* years" in the future, it seems even more inappropriate. Would "Big Began" not be more to the point? But then what is "Big"? Compared to what?

From that singular event, in which matter suddenly and spontaneously erupted from nowhere into being, stars, planets, moons and other assorted stuff were propelled outwards in all directions. Into space one would assume - the *un*stuff that was already there - but not so. Prior to the bang there was nothing at all say the experts – no space, no time, no matter, no energy. Common sense suggests that a singular initiating event would imply a singular point of origin - a center as it were to the universe. Again the experts disagree. There is no center. Everything is expanding outwards but not necessarily from the same place. If pressed for more details these same experts respond that, *"We don't know where it came from, why it's here or even where it is. All we know is that we are inside of it and at one time it didn't exist and neither did we."* This is insight indeed. A caveman could have uttered it and probably many of them did. Aaah, but a caveman wasn't capable of sending objects up *into* this incomprehensible former nothing.

("Space" we were also once led to believe was infinite, prompting yet another painfully plebian question: how can something that is infinite be expanding?)

The answer to all this may rest with Black Holes we're told; hypothetical phenomena where things are sucked back and forth and in and out of nothing on a regular basis - also belying the idea of singularity one would think. Black Holes, Big Bangs and things getting sucked in and out are terms one might attribute to the daydreams of teenage boys who don't get out enough, but they have been bestowed upon us by individuals exalted in the history of human thought. A further indication of their imaginative acumen is demonstrated by some of the means by which they suggest these holes and bangs might be explored.

In the 1970s, Timothy Leary wrote from Folsom Prison about humans needing to escape from the Earth and suggested ways in which they might overcome the difficulties of crossing the vast distances involved. He proposed a cigar shaped spaceship powered by atomic explosions blasted against two enormous spheres suspended behind it. Leary's preoccupations can certainly be attributed to a guy who didn't get out enough, but the precedent for the idea had appeared in *Physics Today* in 1968. An idea proposed by physicist Freeman Dyson - complete with diagram.

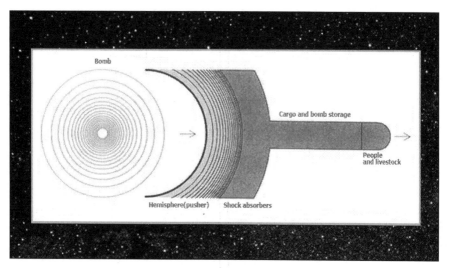

This is not science fiction...

This is science fiction...

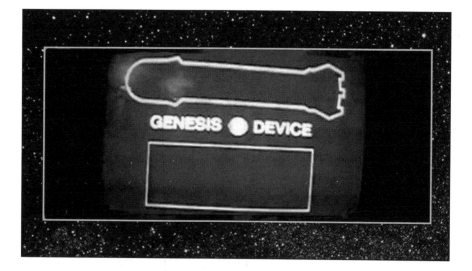

Such unabashed means for *penetrating* the mysteries of space are in stark contrast to the reluctance to owning up to having sexual parts at all. In the 21ˢᵗ century, the discrepancy is still very much with us.

The New York Times illustration above of our female ancestors, accompanied an article in the Science section of the paper published in 2003. It described the way in which we humans lost our hair – or as Nietzsche might have it – how our hair lost itself. The fear of offending readers over their Sunday coffee and croissants resulted in nipples and pudenda being painstakingly obscured by branches and smoke. In keeping with that idea, Facebook started removing images of mothers breast-feeding in 2008. In response to protests, they revised their policy to allow breasts in *"the act of feeding"* … but not simply hanging out for no reason. Loitering with intent as it were. The audience of Facebook includes minors after all, who must be protected from stumbling upon an image of something they were once intimately familiar with and in fact depended on for life.

What characterizes both this moralizing perspective and the so-called more enlightened view of science is ardor. A passionate sense of what is *right*. Adamant, disparate convictions held by individuals and groups of individuals who feel compelled to enlighten others and would surely insist they be included in any delegation that reaches out to equally enlightened folks elsewhere in the cosmos.

This contradictory, gung ho, mish mash of religious dogma, scientific elitism, and out and out adolescent fantasy is what we will take with us to explore - and in all likelihood wreck - other planets;

it is what we will extend as our calling card to other forms of life. Our treatment of the other life on *this* planet is a fairly good indication of that. Other life that we essentially dismiss in terms of "intelligence' simply because no matter how much we talk to them... they don't talk back. This is what is implicit in our quest for life out there it seems: the idea that we can sit down and chat with other folks about what it's all about. In light of our behavior, our fellow Earthly organisms give the surest indication of intelligence precisely *because* they don't talk back. Like the other guests in a hotel full of unruly, conceited, destructive *rock* stars they may be patiently, silently waiting for us to leave.

"The world of animals" said Lamartine *"is an ocean of sympathies from which we taste but a few drops..."* an idea not lost on Arthur C. Clarke, another proponent of the search for extraterrestrial intelligence. At the World's Fair in 1964 he laid down predictions for the future of human progress and some ideas for animals as well...

"With the use of genetics and our present knowledge of animal psychology we can certainly solve the servant problem – with the help of the monkey kingdom. It's a scandal of which we should be thoroughly ashamed that prehistoric man tamed all the domestic animals that we have today – we haven't added one in the last 5,000 years. It's about time we did so."

Science for all its non-religious claims is steeped in the metaphors and terms that comprise it. "Dominion over the animal kingdom" and "shame" are part and parcel of the overall conviction that we are not only in control of our own actions but everything else's as well. From Galileo to Newton to Bacon up through Sigmund Freud, the 'messianic' compulsion to bring enlightenment to the world has derived from creationist doctrine. In the case of Freud, it merely replaced original sin and holy confession with the 'scientific' theory of repressed sexuality and the psychoanalysis couch. Like others before him, Freud was also obsessed with the quest for a single theory to explain everything. A *"single key"* as he put it" *to open every lock."*

Stephen Hawking, the Delphic oracle of our time, is another advocate of this single theory idea – and is also onboard with the search for intelligent life in space. In a three-way discussion with Carl Sagan and Arthur C. Clarke, in the 1980s, he prophesied with characteristically, wild-eyed conviction, that *his* unified theory - which will explain how *"everything* works" - would conceivably be arrived at by the year 2000... always supposing we don't *"blow ourselves up"* before hand. (A concern shared by Arthur Clarke and Sagan both.)

It's 2014 now and so far not a twitch either way. What's key, is that it's the same "we" that's in charge, no matter what the outcome. The idea that there is a majority of life on the planet that doesn't subscribe to the Judeo/Christian/Scientific, progress-driven mindset – or that something entirely *'un*scientific' and/or, *un*religious might happen instead - is not a consideration. WE have simply got it going on. In a few more years WE may know everything.

It's easy to imagine three equally clever Romans sitting around the dinner table having the same conversation:

"Look at us! Technology, culture, law, economics… there's never been anything like us. We've got it going on! We're on the edge of something even bigger, I know it…"

"Knock, knock!"

"Who's there?"

"Visigoths!"

Whitey wouldn't take a *bath* for another 1200 years.

The flip side of all this is the possibility that we may announce ourselves to something even more screwed up than we are. Given our serious psychological difficulties, sending buckets of goodies out into space might be tantamount to the Maya sending ships across the Atlantic in the 1400s loaded with gold and jewels and pictures of themselves in sarongs and sandals. Along with a note of course:

"Hi there…we're here…give us a call sometime… stop by even…"

If that were the case, when it's all over, the otherworldly visitors might leave *us* a note:

"Thanks…and by the way…we love the hat!"

THE AMBASSADOR

Ambassador Jolie visits a refugee camp in Pakistan

"...slow-motion bullets meandering through the air ..."

The first time I saw Mrs. Smith, she was lying next to me on the side of a bus. Later that same day... I spotted her husband on the side of another one. *De rigueur* as it is for Hollywood movie stars, each of them had a gun - silver in their case, a fashion accessory offsetting their chic, black evening attire. Like jewelry almost: Brad Pitt held his, Angelina Jolie had hers strapped to her thigh. Together they presented us with the defining image of an elegant, sophisticated, tastefully-armed American couple ready for a night on the town, the image in fact that we'd all been waiting for. Here at last was the pay-off to a media barrage that had endured for months. By now there was hardly a consumer alive who wasn't aware that the making of *Mr. & Mrs. Smith* was the event that had upset Pitt's real life marriage and outed him and Jolie as an item. Now at last we could see what all the fuss was about. The elaborate foreplay was over. Two of Hollywood's most bankable Barbies were finally about to get it on.

Barbie of course is a flippant characterization. Standing on line in the supermarket and thumbing through magazines from *The National Enquirer* to *Time*, I'd learned that Angelina Jolie was in fact a Special Ambassador to the United Nations. A woman hobnobbing with Kofi Annan no less and in her own words, traveling around the world, *"looking for refugee situations to report on."* This was a noble pursuit without question, but one that didn't seem to jive with the picture on the side of the bus – it is after all what supposedly qualified her for the job. It was part of her resume, the way she chose to express herself. It was what she did for a living. What then makes someone who advocates mindless, gratuitous violence to millions, a person qualified to address the needs of victims of real violence around the world?

In *Mr. & Mrs. Smith* Pitt and Jolie play a husband and wife who are contract killers, or as the teaser on the DVD package would have it: *"...coolly lethal, highly paid, assassins"*. The Kennedys, Martin Luther King and John Lennon were assassinated, but now apparently the profession was cool. The 'irony' is that neither of them is aware that they are both in the same line of business. It is a marriage that lacks a degree of intimacy so to speak, and inevitably after *"five or six years"* it leads them to therapy. Watching Brad Pitt and Angelina Jolie have sex is the reason most of the audience is there, so whatever it takes to bring that about is fine. Like the human Bugs Bunny cartoon it is, that 'whatever' is violence.

Pitt's manager, who lives with his mother, sets the tone: When asked how things are going that morning he replies:" *Same old, same old. People need killing.*" It's a fun business obviously, but a little on the humdrum side. To give us some idea of how it works we are then introduced to a half dozen examples of such "people."

Pitt's victims play cards in a 'back room' and their crimes are not specified. They're a mix of Englishmen and Irishmen. With a gun in each hand, like a cartoon Western star, our cool Mr. Smith, shoots all four of them with as much detachment as someone shooting straw bales. He even makes a quip as he's leaving, punctuating the scene with a joke.

His wife on the other hand, at least identifies the nature of her target's crime: "*Selling guns to bad people,*" she admonishes her swarthy, Middle Eastern looking client - reading him his wrongs as it were, before nonchalantly snapping his neck. She wears an S&M outfit to add sauciness to the scene in keeping with the "...*fun, explosive mix of wicked comedy*" we are led to anticipate from the ads.

When the couple is assigned to "take out " the same target, they finally discover they are competitors in the same line of work, at which point the real excitement begins. Each now determines to kill the other, and more wicked comedy erupts in their home. The ensuing firefight results in the interior of the house being demolished and when the ammunition runs out, the couple resorts to kicking and punching one another. (I am told that prison inmates in upstate New York *love* this film. "*They know it off by heart.*") One memorable scene has husband Pitt repeatedly kicking his wife as she lies on the floor.

They ultimately reach a stand off, guns pointed at each other's faces, which prompts them to realize that they actually love one another. The diddling is over. The audience finally has what it's been waiting for: Pitt and Jolie can get down to business. Unlike the violence, however, which is meticulously detailed in its representation, the sex isn't shown at all. When they're done, the lovers combine their talents to wreak havoc on the companies that employ them. Many people - in the most fun, elaborate and spectacular ways – are killed as a result.

With Pitt in the sack and the film in the can, the Ambassador moves on: flush from her experience as Mrs. Smith, she opts for another cool assassin gig.

Wanted appears to be have been inspired by the way David Beckham kicks soccer balls, the premise being that the muzzle velocity of a bullet can be countered by a flick of the wrist, enabling those with the knack to shoot around corners. It's a gimmick that justifies relentless computer generated images of slow-motion bullets meandering through the air, and in and out of the heads of yet another succession of well-deserving bad guys. Angelina Jolie's role is to explain such tricks of the trade to a dull young "*nothing*" and turn him into an equally ruthless killer.

The idea of a non-accountable, anonymous corporation of vigilantes remains the same, the nature of the evildoers is equally vague, and the methods required to deal with them equally graphic, and unrelenting. On one occasion, a train full of innocent men, women and children is casually wiped out in the interests of moving the excitement forward. True to form, the Ambassador's breasts contribute their familiar 'sauciness' to the endeavor.

Just as it is with *Mr. & Mrs. Smith*, the story is as irrelevant as the plot to a video game or a *Looney Tunes* cartoon. There's no point to the rabbit getting run over by the steamroller or Wile E. Coyote swallowing dynamite, it is simply a pretext for violence. The success of the movie relies on the novelty and degree of the violence involved – violence, after all, is what gets you laid. Spelling that out, however, has its drawbacks, as one exuberant critic put it, *"Fans of R-rated action fare will dig this flashy romp, but the film's manic pace and frequent profanities keep Wanted from being an across-the-board crowd pleaser."*

"Fuck" is profanity. A slow motion bullet penetrating someone's face and emerging in a shower of brains and bone from the back of the head is not.

What do the folks in the refugee camp think about that?

MASTER AND COMMANDER

"...the occasional cannon ball ripping through the kitchen and taking Cook's legs off..."

Obscurantist visual seduction at its very best, confirming once again that conflict among human beings – especially white European human beings - is inevitable, and with the right music, the right actors and the right lighting - great fun to watch.

Like it does in so many action films, masterful, cinematic violence stars yet again in the cause of 'honorable revenge'. In the great American tradition of 'they fired first', manly men bound by a common sense of decency and fair play, battle incomprehensible odds and each other to reassure us once again, that the plucky little guy with guts and smarts always wins.

Russell Crowe revives his Maximus Meridius character for the occasion to play 'Lucky' Jack Aubrey, an early nineteenth century English naval captain, charged with preventing the French from extending the Napoleonic War into South American waters. Of making the war worse so to speak - or bigger as it were. A noble mission, for which true-to-form, officer-who-mucks-in-with-the-lads, captain Crowe is more than qualified. Marshaled against him on this go round are the awful uncompromising forces of watery nature, the unpredictable temperaments of a stressed out crew and the greater firepower of a cunning French adversary. A bigger, boat so to speak - or worse as it were.

A ship at sea is a world unto itself, *"...a little wooden world"* as captain Jack puts it, a microcosm encapsulating all the wonderful foibles and heroic aspirations of the world at large: an 'Upstairs, Downstairs at sea' kind of world, full of the fun and ironic exchanges that necessarily occur between poor people working and rich people giving orders. Punctuated in this case by the occasional cannon ball ripping through the kitchen and taking Cook's legs off. *"Ooh Mr 'udson! Whatever next?" Whereas* the honorable upstairs crowd are clearly defined, each with a name, an ideal and heroic agenda, the downstairs lot are portrayed as an anonymous mob of superstitious yet fiercely loyal slaves. Until the ship needs repairing that is, when despite the fact that such sailors were often impressed into service – ie enslaved – they spring into action with amazing skills of craftsmanship and know how. There is a sculptor on board to fix and repaint the figurehead, a carpenter to fashion a mast from a tree and an uncannily fast model boat maker who is able to pinpoint the weak spots of the enemy ship.

True to formula the hero is the underdog. Cap'n Jack's ship is undersized, underpowered, undergunned and on top of everything else – undermined. There's a Jonah on board, a weak toff no less, who raises the real possibility of a mutiny to top off Cap'n Jack's seemingly insurmountable difficulties. Jack of course isn't called lucky for nothing, and after an evening of getting down on the fiddle with his cello playing ship's doctor pal, he arrives on deck next morning to find the situation has cured itself. Weak or not the upper class has class, and the toff has tossed himself off in the night. With him out of the way the decks are now cleared for action.

Jack is still outmatched but he has one thing on his side that the French ship doesn't: Utterly implausible coincidence. When he's compelled to choose friendship over duty, a miraculous sequence of events suddenly transpires. His friend discovers a stick insect - the stick insect leads to the French - the French lead back to the stick insect - and the stick insect shows Lucky Jack Aubrey how to blow them up. 'Stick' it to them as it were. It's amazing - and a life lesson for the young at heart. In the fight that ensues everyone has a great old time. Arms and legs are whisked away with cannon balls and chopped off with swords, people are shot and crushed and blown up, and all on account of love and a stick insect.

In the glow of the aftermath, all concern and attention is lavished on the individual toffs, none on the anonymous slaves beneath them: the husbands, brothers and sons, the six year old orphan boys volunteered into hell. That they all share the horrors is obvious, but only the privileged are recognized, rewarded and remembered for it.

Jack and the doctor rescue us from such gloomy thoughts, emphasizing once again the virtue of friendship. They turn their fiddle and cello on their sides and send us smiling from the theater with a jaunty, get down, hootenanny jig. The fact that the French ship had not been defeated after all, and that the fun and carnage must be repeated all over again, only adds to the warm thoughts that accompany us back to the parking lot.

SPOKES

"...*parented* to the same spot..."

Scientists suggest they now know how much the Earth weighs. What does this mean?

Each human being walking the Earth embodies a linear force of attraction and repulsion that runs vertically through them, from head to foot and beyond in both directions. Extending downwards it intersects with that of every other human being in a singular ineffable moment at the center of the planet. In computer parlance, all our soles are *parented* to the same spot. Like spokes in a wheel rooted to a single point of origin, each of us then radiates outwards to the infinite reaches of space.

How heavy is *that?*

BUGS/LIFE

"The chuff, chuff, chuff of the cello ..."

Director Samuel Orr presents us with a painstakingly beautiful account of the unique 17-year lifecycle of Cicadas. The video is a trailer, a promo, a 'greatest hits' version of the full-length movie to come. It is designed to capture our hearts and imaginations, to stir us into watching the entire story and hopefully ... inspire us to help pay for it. It is an ad in other words, utilizing all the seductive devices that selling ideas involves. The imagery is stunning, revealing the director's remarkable craft and passion for his subject. The framing and editing are precise, resulting in a story wonderfully told.

A superimposed text dissolves on and off throughout, describing the course of the Cicadas' endeavor: an insistent pulse of narrative, *pushing* out the story, *urging* it forward. It is a subtle *driving* force, the heartbeat of the drama as it were, amplified by the tempo and tenor of the music that underscores it.

Without the music it would be a very different experience altogether – the way it is with all movies. Unlike real life that is not played out to a musical accompaniment, film uses sound to coax our emotions into a fixed trajectory of perception. We are told where to look and how to feel.

The chuff, chuff, chuff of the cello and poignant, punctuating, step-by-step minor notes of the piano evoke an engine of indomitable spirit surging forward; the violin sawing out strains of tragedy and triumph as the miracle unfolds. Against all odds these determined little creatures scramble towards life's sublime reward, its truest joy: a soul mate, "love", continuation. It is an apotheosis, an ascendancy, a transcendence even. The music stirs up our own sense of indomitable spirit, the triumph of the *human* endeavor: families, tribes, nations striving against all odds to continue. Surely our own years of waiting in the "dark" will also finally be justified.

But in what sense is a Cicada's life justified? 17 years underground isn't so remarkable. Many life forms, including some mammals, experience their entire existence this way. They've been doing it without respite for millions of years and in all likelihood will continue to do it for millions to come. Life is just plain weird for everyone.

What distinguishes the Cicadas is that they *emerge* from solitary darkness into *our* world of social interaction and light. It is our indomitable tendency for anthropomorphism that gives them their appeal. We view them within the context of our own desperate need for miracle. Like the cliché associations between particular feelings and musical tone, the cliché associations between darkness and light and death and resurrection are evoked. It's a religious transformation comparable to the raising of souls from earthly internment to heaven. In keeping with the times it is an image of hope.

But it is also an image of stark conformity, a more tangible representation of our current condition. It is an image to be feared. In a time when behavior is being more and more controlled, when uniformity of ideas and purpose are being increasingly enforced from 'above' - politics, history, culture, even our appearances - the music and images strike a base chord of despair. Even the video *itself* has controlled and manipulated our feelings. Social conformity results in precisely this form of insect-like, machine-like, undifferentiated totalitarian mindset. In that scenario, only that which does the controlling benefits.

As much as the spectacle of the Cicadas seduces us into awe and wonder, the roots within us that extend far deeper than the earth, become mindful of their unattachedness, their fundamental insecurity. We know this story only too well:

Darkness into light ... a gloriously fragile perfunctory loving ...an inexorable dwindling of material self ... light back into darkness.

Round and around and around.

UGLY IS

"…the country vernacular for a compliant horse or cow…"

The "Ugly Spirit" was the impetus for William Burroughs' writing career. He attributed the accidental shooting and killing of his wife to the influence of such an elemental force, and his vast output of literary and artistic endeavors was the result. Unquestionably, this body of work placed him among the great visionary minds of the twentieth century.

As with many other artists and writers throughout history, who have also been creatively compelled, or at least re-routed by the suffering of those close to them, Burroughs' career raises the philosophical dilemma of "moral luck": the question whether or not behavior destructive to others that results in 'art for the greater good' is somehow morally less reprehensible. This is especially relevant when the concept of 'forces beyond one's control' constitutes an essential element within the work itself.

By proposing the extenuating circumstance of an "Ugly Spirit", Burroughs makes his role in the event seem less overt. He casts himself as unwitting accomplice almost, as victim even, and the idea of his having to *write his way out* can be viewed as a kind of penance, a form of atonement. In light of his methods, this is a fascinating irony. He dedicated almost his entire literary career to promoting the very elements of drugs and guns that had contributed to the event and he consistently contended that *"...women were a biological mistake."* He also claimed that he often *intentionally* invoked so-called demonic entities as *aids* to his work.

These apparent contradictions are intrinsic to his worldview: "Control", "being controlled", "luck", "chance" "ritual violence" " and "evil influence" are clearly elements that inform his work, but they contain within them a larger idea.

Implied in this scenario is the concept of sacrifice: the 'regrettable fact' that some must suffer in order that the greater good prevail. The Judeo/Christian *and* Mayan worldviews both incorporated sacrifice as necessary and justifiable for the promotion of their agendas, and both included a version of this same "Ugly Spirit" routine. Burroughs in effect, extrapolated his personal experience into the greater experience of the world at large. Sacrifice, particularly the sacrifice of youth, and its promotion and justification by the Biblical/Darwinian driven status quo, is a feature of *Ah Pook is Here, Naked Lunch* and his fiction in general.

Contrary to the idea that Darwinism undermines religion, it essentially endorses its basic conceit; the notion that human sensibility is the supreme evolutionary achievement and the "survival of the fittest" are fundamental to both. Religion merely introduces contrary forces in the form of evil that create obstacles to this dynamic. Anthropomorphosizing this energy into demons and devils makes the concept accessible to a larger audience – particularly children - who must be indoctrinated ASAP.

Demonic possession is not a new idea. The claim that forces beyond our control compel us to act 'out of character' has been accepted throughout history by many cultures. "The Devil made me do it" is a well-worn line of defense. But what exactly is an Ugly Spirit, how does one confront it and to what end? How does one contend with a power of that supposed magnitude? Is it something that can be appealed to and appeased? In bowing to it, as it were, are we anticipating some sort of benefit or dispensation, some level of assistance, the way we do with the other side of the good-evil equation? But what can evil possibly have to offer? It cannot lessen our personal quota of it, because that would be contradictory to its essential character. Nobody in his or her right mind would want more of it because evil by definition is chaotic, painful and remorseless. It cannot be predicted or controlled.

So why would the many black magic practitioners throughout history want to invoke such an idea? Why would Bill Burroughs who was "struggling" as he put it, to come to terms with such a thing, deliberately attempt to bring it – or its cronies - *into* the world... into the *house* even? In describing his painting methods he referred to his muse "*... Humwawa, Lord of Abominations ... his head a mass of entrails...*" who would arrive with his brother "*Pazuzu Lord* of *Fevers and Plagues"*, whose *"...breath [was] the stench of dung and the perfume of death..."* A fun pair apparently, whose company and influence he appeared to derive pleasure from.

In a sweat lodge ritual, he succeeded in actually seeing his adversary..." *a spirit with a white skull face, but no eyes, and sort of ...wings.* "A human form in other words albeit blind, but with the ability to fly. To his guide, getting the evil from 'in *here*, to out *there*' was an achievement. An adversary when seen, said Burroughs, is disarmed.

It is here that the notion of Ugly Spirit appears to diverge from its more profound implications and takes on a more conventional fictional interpretation. The notion of moral luck considers the possibility that none of our actions may be culpable - or praiseworthy - since they are entirely contingent on genetic, environmental and circumstantial influences beyond our control. Assigning a form to that idea, particularly a conventional form of evil, completely reduces its significance. Moral luck involves the question of free will and this it seemed was a fundamental part of Burroughs' ongoing literary enquiry: the debate between a predetermined Word/Image track as he called it and the possibility of being free moral agents. Describing the forces countering free will in such Marvel comic book, bad-guy terms diminishes the idea, certainly if proposed in defense of a crime.

Apart from their changing shape, what makes these and many other embodiments of evil interesting is that they *do* in fact have bodies; bodies that incorporate all-too-familiar aspects of the human experience. They are generally unpleasant, distasteful, foul often disfigured or distorted by facial and/or bodily decay. All the bad aspects in other words, sometimes cobbled together with details from other 'unpleasant' life forms such as bats, rats, rabid dogs, snakes, reptiles, spiders and bugs etc. The conventional representation of the Devil is a goat-headed individual, and it also apparently smells bad.

To describe living humans with facial or bodily disfigurement as evil would be outrageously un-PC, yet this lingering throwback to medieval times is still the vogue. Associating evil with animal characteristics is also atavistic. Evil, both in 'fact' and fiction, is invariably nevertheless cast in this mold.

In keeping with the notoriety of goats, the Devil above all embodies sexuality: rampant, indiscriminate and invariably violent. Sex is the element that appears to unite most personifications of evil and forms the basis of the manner *by* which and *for* which they are sought after. Rituals involving naked adherents in orgiastic frenzy are part and parcel of the summoning process. "The Great Beast" and occult 'magician' Aleister Crowley is revered on that account for his theatrical use of sex to conjure up otherworldly insight. In the long run, however, the insight seems more to do with control of this world than any other, in which respect his 'eenie, meenie, minie, mo' routines don't hold a candle to the likes of Charlie Manson or Rasputin When it came to manipulating the ladies, these guys were in another league altogether.

Crowley went for the conventional kinky stuff: having women actually have sex with animals, eat excrement, have the kids watch etc. That was what made him so popular with his voyeuristic, tabloid reading audience. But what was actually invoked by these shenanigans? Where was the MAGIC? Sticking 'exciting' objects into a vagina produced what exactly... besides a hardon for the master of ceremonies?

(Burroughs refers to Crowley on occasions and they appear to be connected in their numerological obsessions as well as their demonic preoccupations. Burroughs almost has the patent on 23 his "...number of death" and it permeates his fiction. Crowley on the other hand adopted 666 as his nom de guerre - the number of the devil. Between them they appear to have nailed it: The earth's axis tilts 23(.4)° from vertical leaving 66.6° leftover - clearly the Earth is *thoroughly* evil)

Sex with animals is hardly remarkable, it's been part of the human experience since the get go. The hybrid monsters described throughout history are surely the imagined progeny of such romantic liaisons - even the Gods did it after all. One of the great questions of anthropology it seems, is whether men had sex with horses *before* they figured out how to ride them or vice versa. "Stump broke", the country vernacular for a compliant horse or cow, has conceivably been with us a long time. (The term for animals that will back up willingly (so I'm told) whenever a man stands on a tree stump with his pants down.) Kinsey reported - in the twentieth century - that between 40 and 50% of males interviewed in rural settings admitted having had sex with the livestock. It was Christianity that put the damper on that sort of thing and then only in fits and starts. Anxious to maintain the distinction between lowly animals and exalted humans, church 'fathers' began patrolling the sex boundary early on and obviously it was crossed sufficiently often, or the need wouldn't have arisen.

Initially it was simply frowned upon as a boyish (or girlish) habit that would eventually be grown out of, but as the perception of animals changed, so did the perception of the act. Punishment for bestiality was once on a par with that for masturbation and homosexuality and was included among the many rules in the Old Testament Bible. The animals involved were also considered culpable and sometimes also punished. With that, the line between us and the rest of the world became uncomfortably blurred and the practice gradually subsided. The invention of fables also served to lessen the distinction, since animals became imbued with very human characteristics.

In the twelfth century, all that changed. When the fine ideas of hell and purgatory were invented, the possibility of evil animalistic spirits moving back and forth between here and there became an obvious corollary. If human souls were substantial enough to be rogered indiscriminately in the after life, then the devils that did such things were also conceivably substantial enough to do the same thing in this one. The concept of inter-dimensional demon traffic was officially established and bestiality became one if its popular inroads.

Punishments for sex with animals became that much more severe as a result. The concept of "witches" and their "familiars" was suddenly the justification for sexually abusing, torturing, and murdering women all over Europe – and the Americas. Women as the conduit to life were obviously in the front line when it came to blame for the evil in the world. They were vulnerable, weak, easy marks for the Devil - *mistakes* even. They were so 'crazy' they blamed one another. And with the crusades, a hundred years war, a mini ice age and umpteen rounds of bubonic plague thrown in, there was plenty of evil to work with.

But that was our superstitious past.

During the "Satanic panic" of the 1980's and 90's, daycare centers in America doubled as covens for *twentieth century* devil worshippers: mostly elderly women accused of a catalogue of evils from sodomizing little children, to... *"flying"* unaided... chopping off *"a baby's head"* and making a child drink its blood... taking a child *"in a plane to see goat-men"*... forcing one to *"ride naked on a horse on*

the beach"... taking pornographic pictures... and of course dressing as *"witches."* A wide spectrum of obscenities eagerly lapped up by judge and jury and a media ardently fanning the flames. Just as they'd done in the good old days, inquisitional experts scrupulously photographed and examined the children's sexual parts for signs of the devil's ingress and egress.

The McMartin Daycare Case was the longest criminal trial in U.S. history. By the time it went to trial - four years after the first complaint - it had employed "...3 fulltime DAs, 14 investigators from the DA's office, 22 task force officers, 2 fulltime social workers,

20 part-time social workers, a fulltime detective and 4 part-time detectives. They had searched 21 residences, 7 businesses, 3 churches, 2 airports, 37 cars, and a farm, but had come up empty-handed. They had interviewed 450 children and 150 adults and conducted lab tests on clothing and blankets, all to no avail. They had excavated the schoolyard looking for tunnels that the children had described, but found nothing. The true victims spent years behind bars for evils they never committed, received death threats, were assaulted, were terrorized in prison, and had their school set on fire. The local church militia touted placards saying the ringleader "...*must die.*"

Ten years later, in the wake of the Columbine shootings, Bill O'Reilly interrogated Marilyn Manson also on the subject of corrupting children. In his guise as "...*reverend in the Church of Satan*" and with his "*lewdness*" on stage, surely he must accept some responsibility for the evil abroad? Manson respectfully, calmly dismissed the idea – paternally almost. " "*But why,*" pleaded O'Reilly," ...*why the eye, why the nail polish...why the bizarre presentation, which can be misinterpreted?... those lonely kids...tend to gravitate to people like you.*" They should of course be gravitating towards the likes of O'Reilly: God-fearing men who see nothing at all bizarre in their own presentation. As if a jacket and tie and shiny shoes and hair combed in parallel lines to the sides were the absolutely irrefutable statement of normalcy and reasonableness. A uniform that surely attracts equally lonely kids to its ranks: kids who will grow up to rig elections, crash banks, push psych drugs to kids, order drone strikes, bomb women and children...

Who grow up to actually see evil in the form of *form*.

We had it right when we were kids: in dark rooms, under the bed, in the woods at night, it was *there. Without form,* terrifying. It was waiting before we got here, it will be here when we leave. If you see it you disarm it said Burroughs, but it cannot be seen. It has no face. We gave it one. We dressed it up, like a doll, gave it shape, gave it names, gave it sex, assigned it friends, every one of us differently according to our needs. It is the opposite of everything good we told ourselves – what is good for me, what is good for us.

But every idea exists by virtue of what it is not. Without evil there can be no good. If one goes they both go. Black/white, male/female/, life/death, it is both or neither.

In his film monologue *Journey On The Plain,* director Bela Tarr describes human history as a "river of blood". It is an indictment of sorts, a cry of despair, but that is only the half of it. It is also a river of laughter, a river of joy, a river of triumph.

It is both.

Surely *that* is the true evil – the 'ugliness' we must face.

SENTENCE

"...pulled out *through* the bars of our confinement..."

In the beginning was the Word.

Then came the Sentence.

"LIFE"

"The Defendant is found guilty of an undisclosed crime and is hereby sentenced to solitary confinement until the Court sees fit."

"Term is imposed by the Court in absentia. There is no counsel for defence, no jury and no recourse to appeal. The Judge is the sole arbiter accountable to no one."

"Conditions of incarceration are subject to considerations undisclosed by the Court. Termination of sentence occurs without warning based on the same nondisclosure. Escape from these conditions is not possible. The Defendant is both prisoner and prison, any involvement by the Judiciary beyond sentencing is redundant."

"Court is adjourned."

And in the end, without warning, without exception, each and every one of us shall be pulled out *through* the bars of our confinement.

1%

"See how difficult it is to murder a woman this way..."

Marga, says Joseph Campbell, is a Sinhala word derived from Sanskrit. In this, its plural form, it denotes ways, methods and techniques. From the Tamil version of the word, *Markangal,* derives the religious connotation of the Path, the journey undertaken in search of ultimate meaning. To the Buddhists, this search for significance is the idea that each of us enters a Wood in order to discover that which defines us. We follow the trail of an animal, which is the path to the psyche.

According to Joe and the Buddhists, each of us enters the wood from a place of his or her own choosing; there is no pre-existing path, if we discover one, it belongs to someone else.

As it happened, I was already familiar with this idea, but I was not aware there was a religious/mythological precedent for it. I had followed just such an animal into the woods a long time ago and the results had been disastrous. That was the reason I was now reading the likes of Joseph Campbell. The trail I had followed had led me to a place I had not expected and from which I could find no way out.

I started that "journey" after the Sierra Club suggested I write and illustrate a book about Bigfoot - an idea proposed in the sedate lounge of the Algonquin Hotel in New York. My reaction at the time was understandably one of shocked amusement. The Sierra Club was a bastion of scientific enquiry; Bigfoot is a tabloid goofball with as much taxonomic credibility as aliens who advise presidents and Siamese twins who face firing squads for crimes only one of them has committed. It's not exactly Audubon material. I left the meeting smiling and agreeing to think about it. Absurd as it seemed though, I continued to think about it, and over time, the suggestion actually resolved itself into an interesting idea.

The more I read about Bigfoot, the more it started to come alive. Something that began as a hairy galoot shuffling around amongst the roadside trash, transformed into a subtle, ethereal creature as elegant and disturbing as any mythical image that had preceded it. As time went on, I began to discover many different versions of the same idea, a single set of footprints as it were, suddenly splitting into two, then three and four and so on. It became a composite creature, more and more elusive and more and more intriguing. Without knowing it, I was beginning the very journey that Joseph Campbell would later refer to.

By following each of these trails, I was lured deeper and deeper into very different parts of the wood. The paths that were defined led through Zoology, Anthropology, Paleontology, Psychology, Sociology, Mythology, History, Literature, Pop Culture, and

Religion. I encountered Neanderthals, Tarzan, King Kong, Darwin, Charlton Heston, Jane Goodall, Ronald Regan, Nietzsche, and Moses. Just about everyone in the bookstore in fact, from *The National Enquirer* to the Bible.

In the end, all these paths would converge. Consistent with the Buddhist idea, they would resolve into a single *infinite footprint*, in a part of the wood I could not have imagined: a place with no light, no sound, no nothing: a disembodied solitude where all that remained was feeling.

The feeling of absolute terror.

A man in a monkey suit had lured me from the height of comedy to the depths of despair.

Right to the heart of darkness.

Bigfoot, I realized, has been with us for a very long time, in all likelihood from the beginning. It is a shadowy creature wandering the periphery of our world, both fascinated *by* us and terrified *of* us. Not quite like us, but then not like the rest of nature either. It lives in a lost, limbo world, that is why we are so fascinated by *it* in turn, and why we are so equally terrified.

We see it as a possible link between ourselves, and what we used to be, a reflection of sorts, telling us what we *are*, by showing us what we *are not*. Our nearest animal relatives are the great apes:

Chimpanzees, Orang Outans and Gorillas. As science would have it, the DNA difference between us, is very small.

A mere 1%.

It is in that tiny margin that Bigfoot lives, where all its incarnations have always lived: all the human hybrids, all the confused souls, wandering the limbo between what we were and what we've become: the path between not knowing and knowing, the path between comedy and horror.

At the center of the wood there was nothing. Not simply an absence of light, but a place where nothing was revealed. Here was the indefinable *cause of being* - that which defines us all. We cannot determine its purpose, or whether it has purpose at all, and in the absolute darkness, we suffer the *anguish* of knowing that we do not know. It is an anguish that cannot be relieved, because in the light of 'memory', we see the awful methods that inform it.

Anguish, is the impetus of being, the effect of the will to escape pain. Existence operates at the *expense* of life, for the benefit of unknowable purpose. Intellectually this is dismissed as Maya, Illusion - God moving in mysterious ways. In reality, it is the eyes of a child about to be tortured to death.

Pain, and death may be acceptable, but cruelty is the feature of human experience that places it beyond the pale of reasonableness. *Homo Sapiens* is not only predicated on the fear of pain but on the fear of pain deliberately increased and prolonged. This is horror. All religious and philosophical systems fail if they cannot reconcile this reality in a way that a child – every child - can understand.

If they cannot, the result is despair. Life is inherently evil. It is a madhouse where each terrified individual simply tries to stay clear of the horror around them. It is a random system, impervious to personal suffering, determined by an indifferent intelligence, group of intelligences or no intelligence at all.

The question I had for Joseph Campbell and all the other mythological cataloguers therefore, was, even though we start from somewhere different, and follow an animal of our own choosing, do we all arrive at this same place? Is there an inevitable conclusion? And having arrived there, is it despair we are ultimately left with, or is there something else? Is there an awareness that brings light to the center, or is there only darkness?

Must we go insane like Ahab and Kurtz or be forced to fake sanity with faith?

Religious and philosophical palliatives are by definition inadequate if they are devised by those who are merely observing, not *experiencing* this condition. Who are *outside* it, not *in* it. The only valid reconciliation of horror would be that conveyed by those who undergo the process of cruelty to its inevitable conclusion.

Which is an impossibility.

If Giordano Bruno or Savanarola or any of the numberless anonymous souls who have suffered in this way had been able to experience the process, translate the experience into significance, then communicate the significance to those who were inflicting the pain, it would have been contrary to the purpose. It would have demonstrated that the pain was tolerable and therefore inadequate.

Horror cannot be reconciled, yet it functions as the clearest indication of that which separates us from what we presumably were. That is the *infinite footprint* at the center of the wood. How can there possibly be a next step?

Joseph Campbell in his conversation with Bill Moyers refers to the notion of a *"barrier to God."* As a means to overcoming it, he offers one of his many religious anecdotes:

> *"I do not love God,"* says the Indian woman.
> *"Then what do you love?"* asks the priest.
> *"My child"* says the woman.
> *"Then that is God"* says the priest .

That's all very well Joe, but the child she loves, can be destroyed as easily as it was created, and a whole lot quicker than attentiveness and loving made it become. Not simply by a capricious turn of circumstance - earthquake, fire, war, disease, famine etc., but in a manner in which pain is amplified to the degree of horror.

A child embodies the ideas of trust, anticipation, and unqualified joy to a far greater degree than the adult that it becomes.

It is the noblest possible affirmation of a benign instrument of cause.

Yet children have been murdered over and over. This is *my* "barrier to 'God'" Joe. How does the priest explain this? While you're thinking about it, why don't we take a walk - back in time a ways. I'd like to show you a couple of things.

This is the Yucatan. There aren't many trees here, hardly any woods at all. Not a place for Markangal you would think. As it happens though, one tree alone will more than suffice. There is a tree here that can truly lead us to 'ourselves'.

It's a nice day right? Here in the Yucatan most of them are like this. The kind of days you wake up to and say "Yes indeed, there is a God." Those people up ahead have lived here for thousands of years, imagine the sense of benign intention such mornings have contributed to their worldview. But things are confused right now. Something has happened. That is why we're here. Let's consult the guide book:

Yucatan Before and after the Conquest. by Friar Diego de Landa, 1566. Page 25.

One sentence:

"I Diego de Landa, say that I saw a great tree near the village upon the branches of which a captain had hung many women, with their infant children hung from their feet"

One sentence Joe...in the whole history of the world, one line from one of your talks.

Which of these women do you suppose had the conversation with the priest?

I remember you talking about *"feeding the fire"*. You waxed poetic about how life is sacrificed in order for life to continue and how *"perfect"* that is. But then you mentioned being invited to just such a perfect moment- the slaughter of a bull in the Philippines - and when the moment came, you said, *"I had to leave. I chickened out"*

Well the fire has already been fed here. It is over. The *sentence* has been carried out. All that remains is this eerie tableau, like a painting almost; a 'still-life' in the most poignant sense of the word. It's a summary Joe, something you do very well. That is what mythological categorizing tends to amount to: short concise *intellectually* palatable summary. *"Feeding the fire"* though is present tense. In order to *know* the idea, you need to *be there* when the charge is made, when the fire is about to start. You need to *feel* the flames, not just imagine them. *That* is the horror.

We need to come back to this scene about an hour ago, that way we can engage your *"perfect"* moment. You're married right Joe? Of course you are...

One of these women is your wife.

Okay we're back. You're asleep right now, utterly unaware of how the day will unfold, unaware in fact, that days even exist. Such is the numbing disorientating effect of sleep. A day is not rehearsed to our knowing. There are aspects of continuity that we rely on for our bearings, but in all, each day is subject to a vast complex of variables that cannot be predicted or prevented; an inherent randomness that each human being confronts according to his or her abilities.

Are you ready Joe?

Boom! You're awake! Back on set.

Your wife is screaming. Your children are screaming. Everyone is screaming. Men in iron with iron weapons are dragging your family outside: unintelligible, uncompromising, unaccountable beings. God-like as it were.

Why are they doing this? What do they want?

You can't understand what they are saying. You are powerless.

Truly you *are* in the presence of God.

These men have not rehearsed either. They drag women and children towards a tree, but there is no practiced manner in which to do what they have in mind. It is a deafening, clumsy, unruly process.

Your family is far from you now, screaming and huddling with the others.

The screaming that will not stop until this is over.

Your father, your brothers, your friends can do nothing. They have horses, guns and steel, these beings. They have greater *fire*power and they are resolved: the innocent must be expended in order to further their agenda. They must be *sacrificed*.

The men have ropes. One climbs a tree.

The sun is shining. Everything seems so familiar. The tree is familiar. You climbed it a hundred times when you were a boy. Now, a young woman has been hauled up into its branches by her neck. She hangs there struggling, gagging, strangling. You watch uncomprehending as the spasms take forever to subside. You know this woman Joe. You know them all. Then another is dragged forward, her child torn from her arms and thrown to the ground. *Your* child Joe. The rope is forced down over her head and she's pulled into the air. The screaming shuts off in her throat as the rope clenches tight.

See how difficult it is to murder a woman this way. She flails and thrashes to hold onto life. She struggles desperately to loosen the rope. She looks in vain to her family spinning below, her child on the ground, her husband, her brother, her sister hanging alongside her. How does it *feel?* That brief moment when your eyes meet.

But it does not stop there. One woman after another is hauled up into the tree this way until finally the tableau is achieved. Until the *"many"* dead mothers are swaying over the heads of their loved ones like it says in the book. At what point do you think it was deemed sufficient Joe? What determined this number?

You cannot answer. These beings are unintelligible to you. Right now you are unintelligible to yourself. You are numb. But the sentence is not complete. There are eight words left, eight small words. No big deal in the history of the world, nothing at all. Four and five of those words are *"infant children"*.

Infant children dragged crying and screaming by their arms, their legs, their hair. Ropes placed round their tiny necks - each one watching the other in bewilderment and terror - some of them too small to comprehend at all. And each is allocated a mother's foot from which to be hanged and strangled. Do you suppose these men are deliberate enough to assign mothers and children correctly? Do you think in amongst all that dust and screaming and tiny flailing limbs, a moment of reason will prevail? Clear enough to ensure a hanged child would be tethered to its own hanged mother?

It's hard when you can't run huh Joe? When you can't *"chicken out"*. This is your own wife and child not some bull in the Philippines, and you *cannot* even close your eyes. *If you do, they will kill you.*

And when it stops then what? When we are all assembled around this obscene concoction, staring vacantly up at the gently swinging mothers and children. The dust has settled now, the breathing has slowed. The breathing: that which cannot be conveyed through anecdote. Fear, laughter, life, all on the breath, entering and leaving the body.

Do they laugh these men? Do they say anything at all? And what will happen now, now that these human souls have served their purpose? Will they allow you to bring them down, or will they insist they remain there? Day after day, after day, while almighty God with his sun and birds and insects reduces them to vacant featureless trash.

"Sacrifice" right? *"Perfect"* right?

The tree stands there for all eternity. Stands *here*. Here with countless millions of other trees supporting countless other obscenities firmly rooted to their uniquely perverse moment in time. Entwined, impassable, impervious, *indelible.* The Wood, stretches to infinity, past and future. 1% is a number so vast we cannot comprehend it, yet that is only the *difference.* How much more incomprehensible is the *same*?

CADIZ

"George was a dancer not a military man …"

George Villiers, The Earl of Buckingham, was a 'favorite' of King James I. *"God bless you, my sweet child and wife,"* crooned James," *and grant that ye may ever be a comfort to your dear father and husband."* When James died, his son Charles picked up where dad left off. George had impressed himself upon Charles when teaching him to dance.

In 1623, the couple traveled to Spain to convince the king to give his daughter to Charles in marriage, but thanks to George's *"crassness"*, the trip was a failure and they returned to England in a slump. They decided an expedition *against* the Spanish, in the 'glorious' swashbuckling style of Sir Francis Drake, might cheer them up.

An invasion force was duly arranged.

England had no standing army in those days, so men and boys were rounded up as the need arose. For the majority it was a death sentence: fathers and sons herded off without recourse or appeal, to face unimaginable violence and slaughter, or a slow death from starvation or disease. Of the 12,000 soldiers Charles sent to Germany in 1624, almost 11,000 died without firing a shot.

No organized army meant no organized training, and no organized system of supply, but organized contractors made a killing, short-changing food, uniforms and equipment. Starving soldiers often fought barefoot and those who survived – many maimed for life - were often never paid. Those in command got the job through social standing, not military know-how, and they in turn skimmed off more government money at soldiers' expense.

Such a 'glorious' arrangement set out for Cadiz in 1625: 15,000 men aboard 100 ships under the now "*Lord High Admiral Buckingham*"

George was a dancer not a military man, so he assigned Sir Edward Cecil to take charge. "*Battle hardened*" Cecil had been fighting for the Dutch, and he did know a thing or two about soldiery, but he knew next to nothing about boats. Boats could be as bad for soldiers as battlefields. Losing half an army at sea from lack of food and water or disease was not unheard of.

Much of the fleet went astray in the English Channel due to storms, and when the remainder arrived in Cadiz, it was too depleted, too late, and too disorganized to attack the Spanish treasure galleons - which came and went as they pleased.

The town was unexpectedly well fortified, but Cecil ordered his *"rabble of raw and poor rascals"* ashore to confront it ... *without any food or water*. In an inspired military moment, he told them to make use of the local wine warehouses instead, then, once they had become utterly drunk and unmanageable, ordered them back to the ships again.

At which point the Spanish attacked and killed the lot of them.

Cheers.

Two years later, George tried to make good by relieving the *French* town of St. Martin de Re near St. Rochelle. After a clumsy start, the English force finally attempted to scale the walls, but the ladders were too short. Of the 7,000 men and boys that set out, only 2,000 survived.

C'est la guerre.

George and Charles went back their balls.

STILL TIME

"...level the playing field, get rid of the stinkin' rich..."

Two Englishmen walked into a bar...

"Chaos mate, it's total fucking chaos. They're choppin' each other's 'eads off... runnin' around with 'em on sticks. I'm tellin' you... it's gonna get worse and before you know it, they'll be over 'ere..."

"Do us good pal, level the playing field, get rid of the stinkin' rich..."

"It's anarchy. It goes on much longer, some tough guy will move in and take over the whole fucking mess..."

"Not this time pal, this time it's different. This is about Equality! No more rich, no more borders, no one better than anyone else...."

It's the *urgency* that's impresses you, the desperate need to figure it all out while there's *STILL TIME*.

The first guy was right: Napoleon moved in on the equality and destroyed Europe. Hundreds of thousands of men and boys were forced into murdering and maiming one another on an unprecedented scale: 65,000 died in the Battle of Borodino on *one day* alone and 55,000 at Waterloo.

Almost exactly a hundred years later, another two guys were still arguing – one of them again with, "*...this time it's different.*" The same "*Equality,*" same, "*...no more rich, no more borders... no one better than anyone else.*" Stalin took over this time, destroyed Russia, and murdered a hundred million people – including of course, the guy who was right.

EXACTLY one hundred years after that, another two guys were still desperately arguing - Englishmen even. One with the same "*Equality,*" same, "*...no more rich, no more borders...no one better than anyone else.* And again, "*...this time it's different.*" WOMEN were involved this time: they had insisted on *inviting* the tough guy *in*...to help with the equality. Help level the playing field. Help *chop the heads off.* How many dead men and boys will it take this time you think ladies?

There is *always* STILL TIME: a hundred years ... another hundred years ... another... and another...

It is a world of SCALE not EQUALITY.

Keep your receipts.

Talk to the manager.

TOTALLY SIRIUS

"I left a bit deezy" she says..."

The documentary *Revelations of the Pyramids* is a remarkable compilation of data concerning the technological, mathematical and astronomical implications of ancient megalithic stone structures. It is a fundraiser in a sense, insisting that the world pay attention to the potentially dire circumstances these buildings imply, and literally demand more money for investigating them. They warn of impending worldwide disaster we are told, an apocalyptic scenario that we ignore at our peril. The evidence has been there for 20,000 years; it is staring us in the face, we just need to look.

The researcher is a woman and her voice perfectly evokes this sense of urgency. It is a young woman's voice, expressing an inherent vulnerability and its often-frantic tone impresses upon us the sincerity of the message and the terrible consequences of its being ignored. It is a French woman's voice, its tortured English inflections accentuating the feeling of obstacle while demonstrating the determination to overcome it. The fast editorial pacing of the movie evokes the image of a young woman desperately running all over the world, both overwhelmed and overjoyed by her discoveries, while being thwarted by the adamant rejections of established science - the image almost of the archetypical 'damsel in distress.'

The 'cute' mispronunciations and particularly female perspective enhance this idea: *"I left a bit deezy"* she says, *"I wasn't feeling comfortabble, I needed a break... I was tired of not knowing where my informant was taking me..."* Other women could certainly identify with the quality of these feelings, but more significantly with the image of the smart *modern* woman; the embodiment of intellectual female parity and its frustrations in the face of entrenched male academic authority. This woman had traveled the world *alone* amassing archaeological facts like no one who had preceded her, yet her message was being dismissed, ignored, and even derided. By the end of the film I was looking forward to seeing who this remarkable woman was.

The credits rolled by... but she wasn't even mentioned.

The Internet Movie Data Base gave no female credits either that fit her role, in fact, no credit even for "narrator". The author, director, producer and *writers* of the narration were shown but they were all male. After more searching I finally tracked the mysterious woman down.

ALIKA DEL SOL it turns out is a very attractive French actress, not an archaeological researcher at all. As the many online images suggest, an actress apparently known for showing her breasts on screen – pyramids as it were, with their own mathematical, astronomical implications. French viewers of the documentary would probably be aware of this, but the rest of the non French-speaking world probably would not. To them, the first person "I" of the narration - as it had for me - implied that this woman was the actual person who had traveled the world collecting and organizing the information – *and* written her own account of it. That she had not, amounted to an obvious deception, which in the context of a documentary claiming clarity and truth, was particularly ironic.

When a young woman recounts her search for truth, at personal risk, in the face of entrenched, predominantly male academic resistance, it injects an emotional content and sexual element that necessarily skews the narrative. Cute mispronunciations, and breathless references to *"giant structures being erected"*, *"dark passages being entered for the first time, "* and *"the precision of their delicate parts"* take on a whole other character that undermines the viewer psychologically. It 'sells' the idea the way the girl in the bikini 'sells' an automobile. This is a cynical, disingenuous ploy that plays on male and female apprehensions alike.

For males the appeal is fairly direct, but for females it *appears* to confirm absolutely the notion of sexual parity. Here was a woman physically scrambling over buildings around the world, compiling a comparative mathematical summary as sharp and insightful as any man. The fact is, a woman did not do what the documentary implied she did, and it is unlikely she would. Not because she would be incapable of traveling to remote parts of the world and producing an account of it, but because *fundamentally* she would not be motivated by that particular subject to do so.

The fascination with tools and methods of construction is inherent to male enquiry because males have been the architects and builders of physical structure in all human societies throughout history. It is a *genetic compulsion:* males *need* to know how to do it, whereas women do not. To suggest otherwise is to contradict fact and create false expectation. If anything suggests a world in jeopardy, it is the current architecture of sexual deception and manipulation revealed by the filmmakers.

But this is not new: deception and manipulation were here long before we were; it is the madness of knowing that is uniquely ours. The madness in this case of knowing that the millennium-after-millennium onslaught of carnage that humans have been forced to endure, is a much older process than we had previously imagined. Every time we turn over a rock in fact, it seems to get that much older. The film shows us that the madhouse was built very differently back then, but its builders were no less mad, no less despairing than we are.

The creators of this wonderful new catalogue of insanity are simply staking their claim on a particular corner of the same madhouse for their own posterity, using whatever tricks they can to achieve it. Deceiving men and women into thinking women *are* what they are *not* is just one of them - a trick that will be as incomprehensible to the inmates of the future as those of the megalithic inmates of the past are to us.

MONKEY SEE

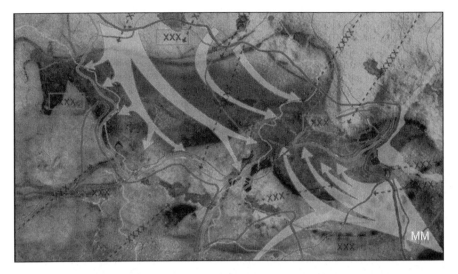

"Female movie 'warriors' are actresses, they quit at the end of the day…"

If we accept the Hunter/Gatherer paradigm, we must also accept the very different forms of attentiveness and perception implicit in each set of behaviors. Given that sexual morphology determines efficiency in enacting these roles, males by default assume the role of Hunters and females that of Gatherers. Each sex in turn, embodies the distinct perceptual mindset relevant to the task.

Hunting is an endeavor concerned with realizing a specific outcome over *time*. It involves *strategy*, the ability to organize behavior based on the hypothetical spatial configuration of objects and events - including the subject's own relationship to them – in the *future*.

It is invariably a *group* venture in which several Hunters coordinate and defer to one another in *physical* pursuit of a common goal. Communication is specific to that intent. The goal is a sentient organism or group of organisms mindful of their own mortality; hunting is therefore an activity, characterized by *stealth*. Stealth involves, patience, concealment, and deception - the ability to represent circumstances in ways they are not.

Hunting entails, physical strength, speed, agility, manual dexterity and the impetus to devise more efficient 'technological' means for increasing the possibility of success. It is a feedback dynamic that constantly strives to update and improve its methods. The drive for *innovative thinking* is an essential, *biologically* determined, Hunter characteristic.

The Hunter is also mindful of his *own* mortality. Strategy concerns success and failure, and necessarily incorporates the idea of *physical risk*. It is a competitive endeavor, not only involving the threat from other predator species, but more significantly, from other out-group human males. The inherent unpredictability of resources makes human-to-human conflict inevitable. Wariness of out-group males is fundamental to the Hunter mindset.

A mutual endeavor involving the possibility of injury or death intensifies all aspects of cooperation, promoting ideas of camaraderie, loyalty, mutual accountability, and altruistic self-sacrifice in the defense of others. It evokes the concept of *bravery*. Hunting is democratic, it encourages *critical* trust and deference to an agreed upon idea. It also results in a particular form of *humor*, a means for sublimating failure, injury and fatality with respect to success and its rewards.

A successful hunt culminates in the death of the prey; killing and pleasure become synonymous. As a realized intellectual and visceral anticipation of future possibility, it represents a tension release mechanism analogous to orgasm.

None of these behavioral characteristics are manifested in the process of Gathering.

Gathering does not involve *strategic* thinking with respect to potential physical risk. It is an immediate 'arms' length' process involving food sources that do not move or reconfigure with possible life or death consequences.

As historical records, and the few contemporary remnants of the Hunter/Gatherer paradigm suggest, women's role in gathering is augmented by the simultaneous need for care of children and other family members. Females represent the locus of the tribe or extended family group around which male activity revolves. *It is the hub to which the Hunter returns.* Both food-gathering and childcare are activities requiring focus on immediate events, unlike the wider spatial orientation required by hunting. It is above all an *organizational* process: the efficient consolidation of food-gathering and preparation, the provision of material comforts in the living/sleeping environment, and the providing of physical and emotional care for all members of the family.

Hunter/Gathering is a cooperative system in which two very different ways of *seeing* compliment and encourage each other to increase the *social range* of the group. The center incentivizes the perimeter to expand and vice versa. Reciprocating sexual/emotional reinforcement increases the drive towards technological innovation on the part of males, as its material benefits increase the freedom of females to extend their organizational range beyond the home. It is a process contingent on biologically determined behavioral *differences*.

Hunters are innately aggressive providers, protectors and innovators, Gatherers, innate nurturers and organizers.

Current attempts to equate male/female intellectual and physical capabilities reference contemporary Hunter/Gathers, including chimpanzees and the Aeta tribe of the Philippines. Aeta women are not only more efficient at hunting we are told, but when they hunt *with* men, the level of success may improve. Percentage statistics are provided as proof! The social dynamic between male and female chimpanzees and the Aeta, however, did not result in the technological means for communicating such statistics. As yet there are no chimpanzees writing computer code and no Aetas walking on the moon.

The individuals compiling these anthropological conjectures are heirs to the European Hunter/Gatherers of Lascaux and Chauvet, not the jungles of Africa and the Philippines. It is the unique conditions of post Ice Age Europe and the resulting male/female dynamic of cooperation that led to the technological benefits and material comforts that allow for these observations.

The search for examples of women performing as well as men implies that such facts have not been considered before, have not been acknowledged, or have even been suppressed by 'male dominated' anthropological history. It conforms to the political agenda that women have only now been given the opportunity to expose these omissions, the opportunity that is, to "...*redress the balance.*" Having 'established' that such a discrepancy exists, it follows syllogistically that women must necessarily be able to participate in *any* activity that had previously been considered a strictly male prerogative.

In her questioning of Defense Secretary nominee General Mathis, Democratic congresswoman Kirsten Gillebrand insisted that he guarantee the continued inclusion of women and LGBTQ individuals in the armed forces. Mathis responded that his mandate was to create as "*lethal a force*" as possible and whatever individuals fit that criterion would be considered. This was clearly not the answer that was needed. "Armed forces" covers a wide range of activities some of which women may be capable of performing, but implied in the demand was that they are also equally qualified for combat roles.

Media and entertainment promote the image of female combative parity. 'Action dramas' show women in armor firing bows from galloping horses and physically confronting men one-to-one. Women do battle alongside men, work high-tech machinery, drive tanks, fly war planes, lead cavalry charges, engage men in fist fights and win. Such ideas have no basis in reality. If there were no differences between male and female physical capabilities, sexes would not perform separately in the Olympics. Would-be female boxing champions would have to compete against the likes of Mike Tyson.

Female movie 'warriors' are actresses, they quit at the end of the day and go *home* to all the conveniences of a comfortable, modern, *secure* female lifestyle: to an environment in which they are *culturally protected* from violence, much less one in which they have to physically fight to survive. A woman who has been protected all her life from being HIT, cannot possibly have the same perspective on violence as a male who has not.

The most efficient members of every military force in history have been males in their physical prime. They are not only physically more capable but also embody *the biologically imprinted aggressive mindset and sense of strategy and purpose that underlies it.* Most significantly, fighting in defense of the group is not an *option* for males. When the 'Mongol hordes' show up on the front lawn, males have *no choice* but to confront them. Unlike females, they have no one else to 'fall back on'.

When an activity is *optional,* it cannot possibly be invested with the same life or death urgency to succeed as that which is not.

In a dire combat situation, a fit, two hundred pound human male benefits most from an equivalent male to support him. There are no human females with those characteristics. In the proposed modern (Western) military, he might instead find himself reliant on a one-hundred-thirty/forty pound female who by sheer statistical probability might be suffering from menstrual undermining, and in all likelihood (also based on statistics) be on anti-depressant medication. The chance that a female will perform at less than optimum efficiency in a combat situation - *even compared to other females* – is exponentially greater than it is for a male. This does not constitute "as *lethal a force*" as possible.

The dismissing and undermining of essential male differences begins with a (Western) educational system more and more predicated on the idea that boys should be treated as unruly, badly behaved girls. They should be forced to comply with the more acquiescent characteristics of girls and innovative non-conformity treated as an anti-social aberration to be demeaned, shamed and corrected – and, if 'necessary', medicated. Competitive sports between males are essential to instilling the values of strategy, group cooperation, winning and defeat, and understanding the limits of endurance and pain, yet the trend is to involve an equal representation of females. Some schools insist there can be no winners at all, since it causes anxiety to those who lose. This may allow for equal female participation, but it also dumbs down the drive towards technological innovation that is integral to the male competitive mindset.

Technological innovation is the envisioning of a possible outcome over *time*. It is strategic thinking predicated on risk: an attempt to improve the means for *cultural survival* in which physical and intellectual wellbeing is committed to an *idea,* even though it may result in failure, humiliation or worse. *For every Wright brothers there are a thousand Wrong brothers*, many of whom die in the attempt.

Innovation is the antithesis of *correctness*. No amount of 'Straight As', BAs, or MAs can simply make it happen. Neither of the Wright brothers finished high school, nor earned diplomas, an idea consistent with many of history's great innovative minds.

Equality of *opportunity* is not equality of means. Reducing gender to sameness, *averages* physical, cultural, and spiritual potential and destroys the mutually reinforcing, sexual dynamic of expansion. It removes the essential *differential* on which all life, all systems for improvement of circumstance depend.

Contrary to *wishful thinking*, the life or death conditions the Hunter mindset must confront have not changed since the beginning. War, like weather, is an *ongoing* condition: it has lulls and moments of extreme violence but it does not begin neither does it end. The Western preoccupation with "correctness" and "balance" is not being embraced by every culture on the planet simply because the planet is not determined by such qualities. It is a reality defined by *scale* not sameness: bigger/smaller, stronger/weaker, faster/slower. To 'disarm' oneself in light of the fact is to arm one's enemies.

Western culture, particularly in Europe, is now faced with the most acute military threat since the Second World War. Compromising the *"lethality"* of its response by insisting on equal female participation in its military is short sighted. Deliberately emasculating its males and undermining its dynamic of technological innovation, is cultural suicide.

So far, so good

X+WHY

"The permutations are infinite: whatever it is, the joke is on us…"

In a recent interview, Richard Dawkins was asked if he would prefer to be "*happy*" or "*right*." He felt there was no reason why he couldn't be both, but of the two he would unquestionably opt for "*reality*". To Dawkins, "*reality*" and "*right*" are apparently synonymous. Given that no individual in the history of the planet has produced one syllable of incontrovertible insight into what "*reality*" might be, this could be considered a leap of faith.

Dawkins derives his happiness/rightness from a reality informed by Science and is aghast there are still individuals in the world do not agree with him. In contrast to a system predicated on reason and accountability that contributes to man's well being, *Religion* is an anachronistic, obfuscating catalogue of superstitious fable that undermines it and even threatens our existence altogether. He is on that account an Atheist, or, as he announces to his TED Talk audience - given the urgency of the situation - "*a Militant Atheist.*"

The Religious "*they*" and "*them*" he refers to are presented as a sort of homogenous mass of humanity all pretty much the same, simply less thoughtful than himself, not as clever, not "*intelligentsia...like us*" as he confides to his congregation. In order to demonstrate the prevalence of this unthinking mindset in the United States, he compares its monetary currency with that of the more 'enlightened' British. The American one-dollar bill has "*In God We Trust*" printed on the back, while the British ten-pound note shows an image of Charles Darwin. "*I can't help making the comparison*" smiles Mr. Dawkins.

What he neglects to point out is that the *front of all* U.K. currency features an image of The Queen, the current iteration of a long sequence of unelected individuals assuming absolute authority by "GOD GIVEN RIGHT." More religion does not counter his argument, but the fact should surely temper his smugness.

If not for the entitlement the English class system entails, Dawkins' own family wealth, and his subsequent privileged upbringing and education might not have occurred the way it did. When confronted with the fact that his 400-acre family estate was the result of a fortune amassed through the slave trade, Dawkins responded that the idea his genes in any way suggested inherited inclinations was preposterous. That goes without saying, but his *memes* - the class identification, sense of entitlement and the loot that went with it — were clearly inherited with ease.

Money is very much a part of Dawkins' shtick, and he appeals to his audience to dig into their pockets to help fund his militancy. This does not fall on deaf ears. In 2017, tickets for a TED conference were - "Regular: $8,500, Donor: $17,000. Patron: $150,000.' Most of the three billion *"they"* Dawkins refers to does not wake up to such intellectual financial ease.

Dawkins attended the elite Oundle Public (private) boarding school then moved on to Balliol College Oxford, a trajectory similar to fellow atheist Christopher Hitchens. Hitchens also attended select boarding schools and also 'went up to' Oxford and Balliol College. In an entrenched class system like England, it is an educational path that presumes and assumes all manner of elevated prerogatives. Dawkins went on to marry the daughter of a Viscount and Hitchens went off shooting pheasants and mingling with the wealth and intellectual cream of society. These are rarified worldviews not accessible to the vast majority of English people, much less those on the rest of the planet, but it is the worldview that informs their position.

Dawkins and Hitchens were recently reunited in a two-hour YouTube hunker-down to consider strategy in the face of this threat to planetary stability. Joining them at the table were two Americans, Daniel Dennett and Sam Harris. Dennett also went to Oxford - via Harvard, whereas Harris received his doctorate from Stanford. The combined intellectual power of the four individuals is formidable, the list of books, papers, awards and fellowships incontestable testament to their erudition. They are a godless force to be reckoned with, billing themselves as - *"The Four Horsemen."*

The debate centers round the irrational notion of God and the incontestable rationality of Darwin; Creationist *fiction* that is, versus Scientific *fact*". "*My approach to attacking Creationism is to attack Religion as a whole*" announces Dawkins. This is an ambitious undertaking: Stonehenge, the Pyramids, the Parthenon and Chartres Cathedral were all erected in the name of Religion and they have endured for millennia. If not for Religion, there would *be* no Science. As for those who practice Religion ... "*We should hold their feet to the fire.*" declares Daniel Dennett. "*...There's no polite way to say you've wasted your life, but we have to do it.*"

Science has given us iPhones and drones and men on the moon, there is no question it should be heady with kudos, but the convictions of *The Horsemen* are lofty indeed. Not only the present, but all Religious history are apparently to be reduced to superstitious rubble. Hitchens' bombastic, bulldozer, debating style is appropriately suited to the task: with his constant references to high-minded literary precedent and terms like "*apotropaic* ", "*entre parentheses*" and "*non overlapping magisteria*" thrown in, his erudition is unassailable. There can be no withholding of cleverness if half the world's population is to be disavowed of its sense of purpose.

"*Religion*" remarks Hitchens " *can help people to avoid hubris.*" an idea that seems to have gone over everyone's heads including his own. The situation is clearly not as cut and dried as it appears.

All *Four Horsemen* drink alcohol during the discussion, Dawkins, Dennett and Harris discreetly from martini glasses, Hitchens unabashedly from a tumbler.

He also smokes cigarettes surreptitiously throughout. In light of the 'militant' insistence on the rational over the irrational, this is ironic to say the least. Despite his smart logical bluster, Hitchens might qualify as the poster boy for the *irrational* and Science's shortcomings both.

In the very near past, Medical Science endorsed cigarette smoking; it was not only considered harmless but even beneficial. Sixty or so years ago, English hospital patients were not only permitted to smoke in bed, but pregnant mothers might be seen smoking before going into labor. It was the risk of patients setting fire to the place that finally prompted the process of ending it. Nowadays, there is hardly a Scientist on the planet who does not agree the original claims were in error.

Such a radical about face is tantamount to a *flat earth theory* disproved.

Every generation is prone to such theories: Science also endorsed the prenatal drug Thalidomide during this period and its catastrophic effects clearly proved its convictions to be wrong. Similarly, many of Rachel Carson's environmental claims at that time have subsequently been determined to be inaccurate or false. That is in the nature of Science and its greatest claim to integrity: the process of constantly redefining itself.

It is also one of its greatest shortcomings.

A disproved fact by definition *becomes* fiction, in which scheme of things Science could be described as an ongoing process of uncovering inherent falsehoods. Some facts may simply take longer than others to reveal themselves as fiction – decades possibly, or centuries, or even millennia.

Scientist Rupert Sheldrake, had the temerity in his own TED Talk, to propose this same idea: he suggested that the great constants of physics, even the speed of light, may *not* be constant at all - a presumption that had him summarily banned from TED forever. Excommunicated as it were, with the same rigorous denouncement as Giordano Bruno questioning the Church.

Science has now 'conclusively' determined that cigarette smoking is not only detrimental to health, but also potentially fatal. Hitchens was surely aware of this yet he continued to smoke and ultimately succumbed to esophageal cancer. The connection may be circumstantial, but it is certainly consistent with statistics and medical research. To continue to smoke in light of this is surely irrational behavior.

But Nicotine is a narcotic, an analgesic of sorts, like alcohol, a means for 'taking the edge off'. It addresses the profoundest of concerns. The need to blur, even derail rational thought, is as essential to human wellbeing as the need to constrain it - even at the risk of life and limb. Taking the 'edge' off is at the very heart of the *Religious* impulse.

We are made aware of the operating principle on this planet within the first few seconds of arrival: FEAR of not breathing, FEAR of not eating and FEAR of not maintaining the correct temperature are the three, intractable, non-negotiable conditions that must be addressed immediately in order to proceed. They are the *primary* conditions that will remain constant throughout the rest of our stay. Failure to address them at any time will result in PAIN that will increase until the situation is remedied. Failure to do that will result in termination of sensibility altogether. The forces marshaled against us in this struggle are relentless, remorseless, violent and incomprehensible. As an added indignity, we are made CONSCIOU*S* of the fact at all times. This is the 'edge.'

The edge is *sharp* and we welcome any means for dulling it. Whether literally through narcotic analgesics, or metaphorically through *other-wordly* Religious palliatives, we do our best to distract ourselves from its insistence. Karl Marx made the connection during the appalling conditions of the Scientific Industrial Revolution: "*Religion is the sigh of the oppressed creature,*" he wrote " *the heart of a heartless world, the soul of a soulless condition… It is the opium of the people.*"

Opium is a means for *not* being here, and *not* being here is as essential to human existence as being here. This is the fundamental purpose of all narcotics: to short circuit relentless, rational, logical awareness with an irrational, dissociative numbness. Whether it is from physical pain or mental anguish it is a means for detaching from the "*heartless world*"; a means for 'getting off', that is as old as consciousness itself.

One of the great cinematic icons of twentieth century film was Stanley Kubrick's ape with the bone in *2001:A Space Odyssey*. This was the great 'aha!' moment of cause and effect that conceivably initiated man's rise to technological supremacy: the bone that smashes a carcass was suddenly perceived as a weapon that could be used to smash living competitors.

What makes the image more poignant is that Danny Richter, the actor inside the monkey suit, was stoned on heroin at the time.

Richter explains his addiction and the personal and professional anxieties it caused in his book *Moonwatcher's Memoir*. Unquestionably the combination of 'being here' and 'not being here' inspired a memorable performance, but what makes the image significant in terms of human sensibility, is that the monkey with the bone has another invisible *monkey on its back*. That monkey is the expression of the 'edge' and our desperate need to 'get off'.

But the need to 'get off' brings a whole other order of anxieties: Heroin is addictive and addiction puts us even less in control of our actions, renders us more defenseless in the face of the conditions that confront us. Science has attempted to separate the genetic mechanisms that bind the analgesic and addictive qualities of opiates but to no avail. It is in that fact that the true significance of the image of the ape lies: the methods that we adopt to allay the effects of the incomprehensible reality that assails us, are invariably IATROGENIC: The remedies - including those epitomized by the weapon in the monkey's hand – simply create more problems.

The moment of that event is 'inspired' by the alien monolith, alien in the sense that its source is unknowable, unquantifiable, beyond comprehension. It is an 'aha!' moment', an epiphany, presented in the form of *fiction*. When we cannot know what something *is*, we express it in terms of what it is *like*, that is the nature of fiction, especially the fiction of Religion. Science decries Religion because it assigns a metaphorical agency to such events, yet anything that changes state involves agency, whether it be called force, gravity, energy, entropy, or - God. Such epiphanies are incalculably rare, but they have determined the course of evolution since the beginning. They are characterized above all by the unpredictable, *non-empirical* element of *chance*.

Darwin made a connection between 13 finches on an insignificant group of islands in the Pacific because he *happened* to be there *at that time*, with his particular biological mindset from which to extrapolate. One of the most profound changes in human perception was the result. The theories of evolutionary Science are contingent almost entirely on the items we *chance* to dig up, and much of that is buried under the sea. Given that the discovery of a single human tooth or toe bone can completely redefine our ancestry and pedigree in a heartbeat, our Scientific means for knowing ourselves is woefully constrained.

It was the *chance* banging of rocks that conceivably moved the Scientific ball along, the *magical* process of actually summoning something from nothing. The mesmerizing organism of fire, transformed light into darkness, heat into cold and provided us with the earliest of respites. It relieved us from the pain of cold and gave us Time to reflect. It extended our days, and created a different sense of community. Hearts and hearth became one. It was a seminal moment of cause and effect that evoked Science and mystery both - and with them, the beginnings of greater ineffable fears. Hundreds of thousands of years on the same frictional sparks would allow us to shoot projectiles into one another, and beyond that the collisions of yet smaller rocks would obliterate entire cities in a flash. As it has been since the beginning, the possibilities for smashing human competitors are often Science's first consideration.

The Large Hadron Collider is the latest manifestation of this great banging of rocks routine, the biggest singularly dedicated machine ever built. It is twenty-seven miles in diameter, but by contrast, the rocks it collides are now all but invisible to us. The experiments hope to throw light on the space between matter, but how much light will it throw on the space between Scientists themselves? The matter they investigate permeates the universe, but the system of apprehension that acknowledges it is rare indeed. A human being is infinitesimally small, infinitely more rare yet every single one of them contains *within itself* the vision of the entire universe and the eternity that enfolds it.

It's all in the mind and of that Science can tell us nothing, not *what* it is or even *where* it is. It can point to where certain thoughts and emotions occur in the brain, but as to why they occur at all it does not have a clue. Its methods are tantamount to pointing at the hand of a clock to explain Time.

"X" marks the spot but the "WHY" is nowhere to be found.

Everything exists within the context of Time, and Science with its linear, procedural tick-tock methodology can only amount to a materialistic parochial view of it. No tick is ever longer than the one that precedes or follows it - or bigger, or heavier, smoother, or kinder.

Paleontology is the basis for Evolutionary theory but it merely uncovers the hard parts of history, the bones and fossils, not the soft tissue that really describes us. Without a modern elephant to inform us, would we have been able to envision a mammoth's trunk? Does the skull of a Proboscis monkey give any real indication of its remarkable appearance? How do we know when proto-human females stopped swelling up into *"pink ladies"*, as Jane Goodall would describe them, with *"one pint mixing bowl"* sized rear ends? These superficial soft parts, in turn give no indication of the truly fragile; our *emotional bodies*: the aspirations, hopes, fears and *"sighs"* that are the deeper expressions of what we are.

The *un*reasonable, *ir*rational, *a*temporal reality of dreams also informs our sense of self. It is a state of mind that allows us to relinquish the need for logical thought, and gain respite from the insistent demand for vigilance, strategy and balance that drives our waking world. The 'edge' nevertheless follows us even into this private universe to remind us of our primary conditions: nightmares are as vivid and terrifying as events in our physical reality - even the dead haunt us there. In terms of rational Science these are *fictional* expressions and even though sleep represents a third of our lives, it can throw no empirical light on it at all.

Analgesic narcotics numb us to anxiety, but other compounds provide the means for deliberately accessing alternate states of mind when fully alert. Naturally occurring hallucinogens have induced atemporal states since the beginnings of consciousness, and some cause more profound disassociation from linear thinking than others. More recently, synthetically created chemicals have been able to replicate the process: quantities no larger than the proverbial head of a pin can fundamentally and irrevocably change our sense of reality altogether. Hallucinogens have been integral to many Religions throughout history and the resulting mindsets have also contributed to Science... and ART, the vast area of human expression *The Four Horsemen* hardly acknowledge at all. Interestingly, Christopher Hitchens announced that he had never 'done' drugs and that he knew "*nothing about art*".

Art is not about efficiency and does not concern itself with answers. It is not about linearity, logic or control. Shakespeare, Beethoven, Leonardo and the millions of artists since the caves of Lascaux, have striven to express the transcendent through fictional metaphor. It too is a Religious impulse, the deferential process of acknowledging the ineffable without imposing upon it.

Imagination, wishful thinking and daydreaming are the impetus to Art, Religion *and* Science, the unquantifiable, intangible means by which we clarify the present and anticipate possible futures. They are also the means for preempting and allaying anxiety – particularly sexual anxiety. The final insult added to the list of Earthly conditions is that we must make *more* of them - reproduce ourselves that is, and pass the FEAR on to another batch of unwitting souls.

Sexual imaginings are by definition the expression of the anxieties and frustrations associated with this imperative, and their individually crafted cinematic narratives are unique to each human being. They are Scientifically *immeasurable* fictions yet they contribute to our life trajectories no less than the physical bodies that incorporate them.

The Amazing Randi is another member of the anti-irrational, atheistic militancy, commander in chief of the pseudo-Science Bunko Squad. People who insist on theocracy are simply uninformed, Randi tells us, they do not understand the way the real world works. To suggest Aristotle and Newton were uninformed for including Gods in their worldview is a wonderful presumption. Without them, supposedly, their outlook would have been far more realistic.

Randi has a wager of 1 million dollars that no one can demonstrate a 'paranormal' act on stage *to order* - reproduce empirically that is, an event that contravenes or throws into dispute the laws of rational Science. Many spoon benders and clairvoyant clowns have made fools of themselves in the attempt, but the fundamental nature of atemporal, non-rational events is that they are qualitative not quantitative - and equally subject to chance. They cannot necessarily be made to occur on demand, but this does not mean they do not occur at all. I will wager the Amazing Mr. Randi a million dollars, that *he* cannot appear on stage and get an erection *to order* – much less fall in love.

Emotional resonance is hardly 'paranormal', but it does not conform to the 'repeat on demand' rigors of Science. Trying to guess whether a card has wavy lines or a circle on the back is also a mechanistic, specific-result-oriented approach that has little to do with the implied fields of resonance associated with telepathy. It does not prove one way or another whether the phenomenon is *real*. The same applies to clairvoyance. Because something cannot be made to happen on demand or happens rarely does not prove it does not exist.

"They say there are flowers that bloom only once every hundred years. Why shouldn't there be ones that bloom only once every thousand, every ten thousand years? Maybe we just haven't heard of them up to now because this very day is that once-in-ten-thousand-years." Yevgeny Zamayatin *"We"*

Modern Science acknowledges its debt to the Alchemists, the individuals who first struggled to identify the rules of mathematics, chemistry and physics. But to the Alchemists, Science was merely the *metaphor* for a far greater process: the comprehension, measuring and refinement of the Alchemist himself. It was a Religious endeavor. Newton and the Enlightenment pioneers also characterized their discoveries in terms of an acknowledgement to God; each new understanding being a further glorification of the greater context in which it existed. Over time, however, 'man' became more and more objectified, more and more a material compound devoid of soul or innate ideas. Increasing secularism gradually edged Religion out of the equation, until - as Nietzsche pronounced at the end of the nineteenth century – God was *"dead."*

But as Nietzsche also pointed out, the *need* for God would remain and as he perfectly predicted, those that abandoned conventional Religion would strive to devise other forms of ideological palliative to replace him. In only a few decades, Marx's materialist vision of man would be the first to try. The Bolshevik "*intelligentsia*" defined man as a quantifiable, mathematical entity... a *Scientifically* engineered cog in a flawless machine. In their vision of society no individual would be more or less entitled than another, everyone reduced to a contented number in an equation free of concerns; everyone happy at last.

Science would become the opium of the people.

Trotsky envisioned a future in which, "*...the average human being [would] become an Aristotle, a Goethe, a Marx – and beyond that new peaks [would] rise,*" Over the course of seventy years, tens of millions of Russians would die in the process, murdered, starved to death, or worked to death when they failed to conform to the equation. Not one Aristotle was created. There were no 'aha!' moments. Original thought was heresy. In the words of Mr. Solzhenitsyn – "*... the most morally or intellectually valuable people were extirpated from the population.*" (Hitchens was a fashionable Communist at Oxford, despite the appalling record of carnage it had demonstrated up to that point. He later modified his position, in an intellectual nicety, to being a Trotskyite.)

In keeping with Marx's directive for "*...unbridled militant atheism*", Leon Trotsky was responsible for eradicating Religion in Russia. He organized the destruction of all churches, and synagogues, the murdering of bishops and priests, and closed all Religious funded schools, orphanages, hospitals and charities. It was a *de-moralizing* agenda achieved through brute force and terror that destroyed the ethical compass and value system that focused community. In effect the Bolshevik "*intelligentsia*" replaced the priests they had eradicated. As it happened, they did not subject Islam to the same ruthless destruction. Their reasons were precisely the reasons *The Four Horsemen* now focus their attentions upon it.

They narrow their definition of Religion to The Bible and rate the three interpretations of God it represents according to their threat to worldwide stability. Their principal target is Creationism, the myth that initiates Judaism, Christianity and Islam and the absurdist dangerous mindset it engenders. They do not allow that there is any validity to the myth, choosing instead to simply dismiss it as agreed upon superstitious nonsense. In this they demonstrate the same literal-mindedness of which they accuse their opponents.

Creationism is an astute *description* of the human dilemma – that is why it has endured for so long. It posits the *metaphor* of Eden, an original state of *perfection*. Perfection is an impossible condition, since by definition it cannot *move,* it has no *reason* to move, it is *bound* by its perfection. It cannot change. It cannot evolve. A condition that does not change, in effect does not exist. Change is a relative dynamic, requiring contrary forces - things reacting against one another. In order for perfection to change, therefore, it needs a force to react against it. As the metaphor describes, it is *relativistic* human consciousness that provides this vital ingredient. *Imperfect* 'Man and Woman' react to Eden and bring relative awareness into being. They are 'cursed' by this 'knowledge' and can never return to the 'perfect' state of inertia. They embody imperfection, in order to exist they must forever be wanting.

Science presents precisely this scenario in its theory of the Big Bang: from the impossible state of 'nothing' comes the 'something' of the universe, the dynamic of reaction and change. It is a strictly materialistic interpretation of change in contrast to the non-materialistic human perspective of Creationism. Both views are contingent on consciousness, but what distinguishes them is that Religion admits that words fail us in our attempt to describe the simultaneous possibility of existence and non-existence; its sheer incomprehensibility is therefore simply referred to as God. Science dismisses this term and is convinced it can assign a tangible value to *explain* it.

Given the appalling nature of reality, both Science and Religion nevertheless strive to create some new state of perfection. But as the Creationist metaphor points out, the fundamentally contradictory nature of the idea means it can only be achieved if we are no longer conscious – which will ultimately be the case. Eventually, says Science, the material 'something' of the universe will revert back to the inertia of 'nothing'. Eventually, says Religion, each of us *individually* succumbs to the perfect inertia of death. In order to allay the fearful anticipation of this ultimate state of non-existence, Religion, unlike its material counterpart, offers the solace of PURPOSE.

Lack of purpose, is one of the celebrated tenets of Evolutionary theory, as Daniel Dennett takes pleasure in reminding us. It is a wonderfully Escheresque trick, in which he gives purpose to his own life by saying there is none. If that were the case, one cannot help but wonder why he is bothering to tell us, or why his audience is facing towards him not the other way. After umpteen billion years of it, however, Professor Dennett is finally able to mitigate the quandary.

He compares a termite 'cathedral' with that of Gaudi's Sagrada Familia, in order to qualify the anathema of "Intelligent Design." The evolutionary process has been propelled by chance and expediency, not an overarching intelligence, he reminds us, but finally after billions of years of fortuitous random collisions it has arrived at what might truly be described as *"intelligent designers"*. Those would be *us* no less, *Homo sapiens*, the wise guys, the culmination of all the mindless fumbling and fucking. There is purpose after all and we are it. There are no Gaudi termites, they are merely *"automata"*, Mr. Dennett yells us, theirs is a bottom-up process driven by habit, unlike human endeavors that are top-down, driven by mindful intention. Informed by *'intelligentsia"* that is – *"people like us"*. The *"Anointed"* as Thomas Sowell so aptly puts it – 'Chosen' even.

Science readily incorporates the methodology and terms of Religion - Messianic conviction being only one of them. Apple computers, in the vanguard of Scientific inquiry, take their logo from the *Creationist* Garden of Eden. In keeping with the 'dominion over all other life forms' directive, Arthur C. Clarke was *"ashamed"* to admit that we haven't domesticated one new animal, i.e., created one new *"servant"* (his term) in 5,000 years. In the 'original sin' department, arch panty-sniffer Sigmund Freud converted the Catholic confessional into a therapy couch and used the same kind of 'talk dirty to me' methodology on his patients as the more questionable of his Religious counterparts. In addition to Rupert Sheldrake's excommunication for Scientific 'heresy', the pronouncement by so-called Climate Science that *"there can be no more debate"* is the ultimate expression of Religious dogma.

It is the communication of ideas through language that justifies our exalted place on Dennett's Tree of Life, the process of blowing air across our teeth and vibrating the eardrums of others with considered truth – making stuff up out of thin air as it were. The fact that communication between other life forms – including termites - might not employ such methods, hardly precludes the idea that an understanding of intention does not occur. Science has simply not discovered the 'tools' for perceiving it yet - and there is no telling if and when it will. This is another shortcoming of Science: it is forever short in coming. It may be able to supply answers, but given the circumstances we must endure during the process, the ends cannot possibly justify the meanness.

Science is concerned with answers but as yet it cannot figure out the question. More significantly it has not figured out WHY we are asking it. We are the punchline to an elaborate, consistently nasty joke and we have spent the past 10,000 years trying to figure out the set up. The permutations are infinite: whatever it is, the joke is on us. Stephen Hawking - without a hint of irony - claimed in the 1990s, that by the year 2000, "...*we will know how everything works*". This will supposedly include why we need to know it. Twenty years later there is no answer in sight. In the meantime we have experienced worldwide carnage the way we have always done.

Coincident with Hawkins' pronouncement, the Soviet experiment finally collapsed: the materialist, Scientific, reductionist vision of man had failed. Its successor Cultural Marxism has nevertheless picked up the pieces with its own interpretation of the same obsessions, the same "top-down" ideological convictions that reduce the 'ignorant masses' to a common denominator in the interest of Control. Just as its predecessors had attempted a century before, this rebranded Socialism determines to impose its convictions worldwide.

Its "multiculturalist" collectivist agenda has now succeeded in enforcing the intermingling of *radical* Islam within European culture– and *this* is the real concern of *The Horsemen*. This is the reason for their emergency summit. All agree that Christianity and Judaism have all but lost their virulent edge but in Hitchens' words, *radical* Islam *"must be extirpated."* This is indeed 'militant atheism' - and somewhat ironic.

The Horsemen pride themselves on their successes in thinning the ranks of Judeo/Christianity, but they have made next to no impression on their perceived main adversary. In addition, the Cultural Marxist heirs to Hitchens' very own Trotsky have succeeded in positioning that adversary in the midst of the Democratic Western culture, that made Science – and *The Four Horsemen's* ability to speak freely about Religion - possible. Both *"militant"* Cultural Marxism and *"militant"* Islam are intent on destroying that culture. Neither of them cares for contrary argument no matter how logical, much less to having their God described as nonsensical fiction. They are monologues that resist innovation, unlike reactive dialogue that encourages it. They strive for 'perfect" inertia while Science strives for the ongoing "imperfection" of change. The *"militant atheist"* Light Brigade, with its appeals to right, truth and reasonableness, may soon be literally at war to defend the side of the Creationist myth it decries.

Pestilence, Famine, War and Death: giddy up.

Right, truth and reasonableness are arbitrary, ephemeral ideas, certainly not the determinants of history. In a reality for which no manual exists, where no instructions are given, there is no criterion against which the truth of any idea can be held. If there is no criterion for truth, then there can be no measure for those who claim to know it. If nothing can be known for certain, how can anyone consider themself *smarter* at knowing *nothing* than anyone else?

'Smart' is the ape with the bone, the one with the biggest stick and the determination to use it. *"As it was in the beginning, so it shall be.."* Human against human is the way of things, but what does it amount to in the scope of a spiraling galaxy? What are four men sitting at a table compared to eternity? Billions of *"automata"* will go about their business regardless, the way they have always done, even if there is no Science left to record it.

When a man digs his wife and dead children from the rubble and looks up at a million indifferent stars he asks "WHY?" He does not stop to ponder the magnificent economy of Planck's second radiation constant or Cohn's polynomial irreducibility criterion. He cares nothing for Darwin and his linear temporal follies. He cries out from the *infinite* reaches of fundamental human despair.

"Human history is a river of blood," says director Bela Tarr. This is self-evident. But it is also a river of laughter, a river of joy. It is a river of triumph. *That* is the despair.

God is a 'fiction', a placeholder that has tried since the beginning of consciousness to describe this dilemma. Science is still the Alchemists' metaphor: a means for trying to come to terms with itself, one more device for getting the monkey off our back, for trying to reach the itch we cannot scratch.

There is no 'equals' beyond X+WHY.

The difference between a duck, is that one leg is both the same.

There will always be rubble.

MALCOLM MC NEILL worked as a political artist for *The New York Times*, cover artist for *Marvel Comics* and collaborated with author William S. Burroughs for almost a decade. His images have been exhibited in London, New York and Los Angeles. As a Director, he won numerous awards including an Emmy, and was introduced at the *Broadcast Design Awards* in 1991 as "*...the man probably responsible for the most imitated* [television] *design style of the 1980s*". He has written and published four books.

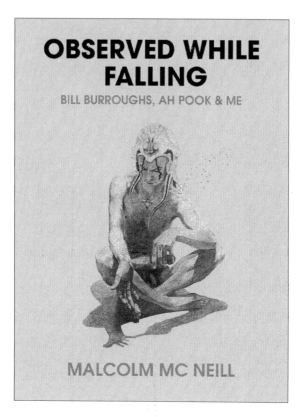

OBSERVED WHILE FALLING

BILL BURROUGHS, AH POOK & ME

MALCOLM MC NEILL

An account of the seven-year collaboration with author William S. Burroughs, on the graphic novel *Ah Pook is Here*, a project that was lost to the record then unexpectedly revived in 2003. *Observed While Falling* was inspired by the English artist Frederick Catherwood, whose uncannily similar life trajectory and own collaboration with an American author in the 1840s, confirmed the original motives for *Ah Pook is Here* and revealed unique insights into the nature of time and the creative process.

FANTAGRAPHICS BOOKS 2012

"*Observed While Falling* presses almost every button: it's philosophy; it's science fiction and it's science fact. It plays astonishing tricks with reality...more specifically, it's an account of the creation of *Ah Pook Is Here*, the great 'lost book' of the last century... a literary case history that belongs on every counter-cultural bookshelf."
HEATHCOTE WILLIAMS: *International Times*

"No one ever produced better images for, and with, Burroughs than Malcolm McNeill. *Observed While Falling* is a sincere, bizarre and moving memoir, and *Ah Pook Is Here* is without doubt the finest extant visual contribution to the Burroughs oeuvre and mythology."
JAMES REICH: *Boldtype Magazine*

"I can't think of anything in the graphic arts that equals its scope and ferocious beauty. [*Ah Pook is Here*]"
TED MORGAN: *Author, Burroughs Biographer*

"The book is great as a concept as much as a memoir...it resonates for anyone who intersects with Burroughs...The Catherwood material I found absolutely compelling..."
Prof OLIVER HARRIS: *Author, Burroughs Academician*

" [Mc Neill] draws an indelible word portrait of Burroughs unlike anything I've read elsewhere."
JAN HERMAN: *Author*

"In a market saturated with books that retread the same well-worn ground in building the legend of the Beat Generation...*Observed While Falling* stands apart..."
CHRIS NOSNIBOR: *Paraphilia Magazine*

"An autobiographical saga by turns as comic as Joe Orton and sinister as Kafka… Mc Neill's Sam Spade-like doggedness in dismantling so many traps and snares to bring this extraordinary work into the light is a cause for rejoicing for all true Burrosicrucians.""

MAX BLAGG: *Author*

"*Ah Pook Is Here*, a collaboration with Malcolm Mc Neill, unfinished and unpublished in its full glory, and maybe because of this fact, remains Burroughs' *Gesamtkunstwerk*, his total work of art.

JED BIRMINGHAM: *Realitystudio*

THE LOST ART OF AH POOK IS HERE: The complete archive of imagery produced in collaboration with William S. Burroughs including a creative overview by the artist.

FANTAGRAPHICS BOOKS 2012

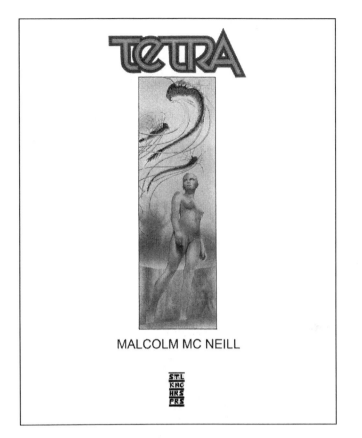

TETRA

MALCOLM MC NEILL

The first-time reprint of the Science Fiction series published by
Gallery Magazine from 1977 to 1979. The author includes an
illustrated account of its creation and the context of the idea.

STALKING HORSE PRESS 2018

Made in the USA
Columbia, SC
10 June 2018